PRAISE FOR

MW01095047

To say that Ern...
today's youth is a m...
of his literary tapes...
McDowell" equivale...

years?), Ernest hits at the crux of the matter affecting many singles today who are craving for the elusive 'happily ever after' that marriage is touted to offer. In this marred world of sin where the stark reality of breakups and divorce seems eons away from the dream of marital utopia, this book sheds a ray of hope to the many disillusioned and broken-hearted singles of today. It is possible to have an immensely joyful and fulfilling man-woman relationship exemplified in holy matrimony as God intended. After all, he is the author of love himself!

Through these pages filled with thought-provoking insights and practical examples, you will discover the Master's divine secrets to making your relationship and marriage work, drawn from principles stated in his user manual: the Bible. What better way is there to drive your future to success than to follow your Manufacturer's instructions? True to its name, *Baesics* takes us back to the basics. This is a must-read for anyone in pursuit of their marriage Eden, where perfect love all began.

—Dr Frederick K Wangai,
Consultant Physician and Lecturer, University of Nairobi

• *Baesics* is well researched, well presented, biblical, and practical. Ernest's humour comes through as he draws on everyday examples to illustrate his points. Men and women preparing for marriage will find that *Baesics* drives them to "know your Master passionately, pursue your mission radically, and you will find your mate graciously." The truth that "you can only attract someone who pursues the same depth as your pursuit" is well illustrated in the book. For those already married and going through a dry spell, the truth that "actions of love will bring back feelings of love" is well articulated in *Baesics*. The idea of "falling out of love" should be a foreign concept to the believer that is already married. This book does a splendid job of presenting marriage between a man and a woman the way God intended it.

—Dr Stanley W. Mukolwe, Founder of Raising Future Parents,
Director of Family Life Ministry at Navigators Africa

I can't think of a more relevant book for our times. In a world that no longer sees marriage as sacred or even particularly significant, this book shines a beautiful light on how singleness, dating, and marriage can be approached in a God-honouring way.

Baesics is written with authority and conviction. The couple's desire to serve their readers in building relationships with a strong foundation comes through on every page. The writing is compelling and creative, with many real-life examples to make it practical for readers. Above all, the book is filled with the words and wisdom of Scripture, setting it apart from many other "how-to" marriage manuals.

I have watched my young adult daughters navigate the emotional difficulties of singlehood and identity, so I was particularly grateful for the book's perspective that it's possible to thrive in singlehood by living a life centred on God. Yet, also for the reminder that "If God could get Adam a mate in a world with no human beings, he can definitely get you one in a world with seven billion."

This is a book I would like to gift to every young person I know (and a few old ones too!). *Baesics* is a deep and thoughtful read which ultimately teaches us to trust God and wholeheartedly surrender our lives and relationships to him.

—Joan Campbell,
trustee of Media Associates International–Africa,
author of *Encounters: Life Changing Moments with Jesus, Journeys: On Ancient Paths of Faith,* and *The Poison Tree Path Chronicles*

Baesics provides a practical blueprint for thriving in romantic relationships. Its first edition left me grateful that I read it before I found my wife. This second edition has renewed the timeless principles that enrich my marriage. The insights and personal stories have helped me to catch the little foxes that ruin the vineyards of purity, level up my emotional IQ, and uproot the idols that creep into my life. It has helped me reaffirm my true identity in Christ, explore the SHAPE of my calling, and clarify God's design and purpose for relationships. I am indebted to Ernest and Waturi for their ministry. There is so much to be gleaned from this book.

—Peter Kamero,
lawyer, leader at Christ Is The Answer Ministries'
Bible exposition service

Are you a Christian with a hunger to run after the Lord's will for your life? Have you battled with dating in a secular world? Have you been thrown off track time and time again but you desire to seek purity and true godly love in a healthy marriage? Then this is definitely the book for you.

Ernest and Waturi are passionate followers of Jesus, and this passion is exhibited in every page. *Baesics* is designed with structured and bite-sized chunks so that the reader can dip in and out, gleaning nuggets of godly wisdom. It is soaked in holy instruction and it provides the bedrock of truth to build your future marriage upon. Clear and concise explanations brings colour and clarity to what the Bible says about marriage and how we prepare for marriage God's way. I have found myself coming back to this book time and time again. I advise all Christians desiring to meet their match to read this one!

—Anna Dawson, Geophysicist, Terrabiotics in London

TESTIMONIES

Praise the Lord! I had to let go of the relationship. I yielded to God today and he just did wonders. The Lord took all the burdens I had. I cried the whole time as we worshipped. I'm overjoyed now. I will let God have his way. I am delivered! I want to thank God for you. May your ministry continue to change people like it did to me. Be so blessed. Thank you!

—I.

Sin graduates. I started with sex to abortion to porn to masturbation and before it could graduate again Christ saved me. I am changed. I sacrificed my relationship of four years to live pure. I had to quit to live right. I feel free and I thank God for people like you who are not ashamed to speak about sex. You are a real inspiration. I have been reading your blog. Keep up the good work you are doing. Now I am getting married next year. I will join in teaching the youth about all the mistakes I made. I will use my scars as a testimony.

—T. J.

Just before I started attending your series on love, sex, and relationships, I was about to go back to my ex, even though he is not born again. I had believed that God had his best for me, but I was just plain tired of the wait. But God intervened by sending you my way. What the enemy had planned for evil, God used for my good. I am glad to pursue purity with like-minded people, especially now that I have made a public commitment to God. Thank you for obeying God in this area.

—G.

I was engaged from December 2014. Oh, I loved this man after being together for almost five years. There was just one thing – he wanted more than one woman to himself. I thought he would change. I consented to having sex with him. I thought if I didn't, he would go out and get it with other women. We broke up a few months before our wedding and the next week he was already seeing someone in my neighbourhood! I had to bear the pain of seeing him drop her off almost every day. They moved in together after barely three months of dating.

Has it been easy? No, definitely not. Has it been amazing? Yes! Because I have surrendered myself to the Master. Isn't the Holy Spirit awesome? I don't blame myself for the things I had no control over. I forgive him and myself too. How I wish I'd had this information earlier! God found me in my brokenness, and he is moulding me into a masterpiece. Now I know what the Lord saved me from, and I thank him daily for that.

It's been three months since they moved in together and my phone cannot rest. He still wants me to be in his life. The instructions from the Lord are clear – don't look back, my child, don't look back. Thanks for the work you are doing. I am a pro in sharing with my girlfriends. I don't want them to go through what I went through. *Barikiweni sana, sana, sana!*

—S.

Thank you so much for writing this book. Truth be told, I am one of those who is struggling with lust and masturbation. It's embarrassing. I feel ashamed every time I say it's over but I find myself back at it again. I believe that this guide will help me and I will finally get over this.

—M.

What a *rhema* word! It has made me shed my tears in repentance pertaining movies and programmes that have unworthy scenes. May God preserve my heart as I have decided never to entertain them again.

—D.

God used you to speak to my stubborn addictions. I got married thinking masturbation would stop, but it did not. I would do it immediately after my wife left for work. It was such a strong force. Through your articles and constant resistance, I am free from the thing. Keep up the good work writing on this. You do not know the number of lives you have transformed. *Asante* (thank you) for allowing God to use you.

—M.

BAESICS

ERNEST WAMBOYE
AND WATURI WAMBOYE

ISBN 13: 978-1-59452-793-7
ISBN: 1-59452- 793-8

Published by Oasis International Ltd.

Oasis International is a ministry devoted to growing discipleship through publishing African voices.
- We _engage_ Africa's most influential, most relevant, and best communicators for the sake of the gospel.
- We _cultivate_ local and global partnerships in order to publish and distribute high-quality books and Bibles.
- We _create_ contextual content that meets the specific needs of Africa, has the power to transform individuals and societies, and gives the church in Africa a global voice.

Oasis is: _Satisfying Africa's Thirst for God's Word._
For more information, go to oasisinternational.com.

The author and publisher have made every effort to ensure that the information in this book was correct at press time and disclaim any liability to any party for any loss, damage, or disruption caused by errors or omissions, whether such errors or omissions result from negligence, accident, or any other cause. However, if you feel that your work was not accurately cited, please reach out to us at info@oasisinternational.com and we will make every effort to review and correct the book where required. Furthermore, any internet addresses (websites, blogs, etc.), telephone numbers, or the like in this book are offered only as a resource. They are not intended in any way to be or imply an endorsement by Oasis, nor does Oasis vouch for this content.

Printed in India

22 23 24 25 26 27 28 29 30 31 BPI 10 9 8 7 6 5 4 3 2 1

RUN HARD AFTER GOD.
IF ANYONE CATCHES UP,
INTRODUCE YOURSELF.

TABLE OF CONTENTS

BAE / 'beɪ / noun *(slang)*

1. A term of endearment referring to one's lover.
2. A person's boyfriend or girlfriend (often as a form of address), e.g., "I'm going to see my bae."
3. Abbreviation meaning Before All Else.

BASICS / 'beɪsɪks / noun *(informal)*

1. Fundamental facts.
2. Principles from which other truths can be derived, e.g., "Let's get down to basics."

BAESICS / 'beɪsɪks / noun

1. Fundamental principles, before all else, to make relationships with the opposite sex thrive.

INTRODUCTION

There is something special about a man and a woman in love. It is so profoundly beautiful such that even wise King Solomon admitted that of the four most wonderful things he could think of, he could not understand the romance between a man and a woman (Proverbs 30:18-19). Men and women were made for each other. Our differences complement each other. Our strengths and weaknesses complement each other. Even our physical bodies fit into each other so perfectly for sexual union.

In fact, few topics arouse as much interest as that of a man and a woman in love. It's the crux of Romeo and Juliet, Beauty and the Beast, Shrek and Fiona, and virtually every famous romantic love story we have ever heard. One man, one woman, and one love. Such stories befuddle us when they don't have happy endings. However, heartbreaks and pain seem to characterize many relationships between men and women.

Turi and I have our inboxes filled every month with hurting men and women who are crying for their relationships with the opposite sex to work. What we teach them, we will teach you in this book. If you are single, this book will teach you how to thrive in your singlehood and prepare yourself for a thriving future relationship with the opposite sex. If you are dating or courting, this book will challenge you to tweak your life in order to get the best that God offers for your relationship with your partner.

Our content is biblical and themed with lots of Scripture because we believe in the supremacy of the Bible as God's Word and we believe in its inerrancy and inspiration by the Holy Spirit. We have seen very clearly in our own relationship and in those of our heroes and mentors, that when the Scriptures are obeyed, men and women experience a deep kind of intimacy and affection that makes the world marvel. They want it as well. They crave to have what you have. What they do not realize is that all we need for life and godliness God has given us and has also revealed in his Word for our benefit.

We also believe that the human being was not made to live for things. When you die, all the money, cars, estates, and whatever tangible and intangible inanimate assets that you have accrued will not escort you to the afterlife, even if they were piled into your casket. You will leave them all on Earth. In your eulogy, how you related with people will be the bulk of your memoirs – more than the toys you had.

When your mother gave birth to you, your first reaction was not a silent ponder over how you would make it through the tough economy of your republic. Nay! Your first reaction was a cry for air and a need for human hands to hold you and make you feel loved. Why? Because you were made for relationships! On their deathbeds, dying people never request to see their bank account balances just one more time so that they may rest in peace. Rather, they ask to see their estranged spouses, children, parents, siblings, and friends one last time. In irrational birth, you cried for relationships. In inevitable death, you will crave for relationships. Have the guts to admit that in between you were made for relationships.

Consider this the start of your relationship with our written thoughts in this book. Even in the prime of your life, no matter how much money you make, no matter how sexually attractive you become, **BECAUSE YOU WERE MADE FOR RELATIONSHIPS!** no matter how fast you rise in your career, no matter how important your job becomes, and no matter how educated you become, you will never really experience a complete fulfilment in your soul if you have all those things, but your relationships are failing. <u>We weren't made to live for things; we were made for relationships. We don't need things to enjoy life; we need life to enjoy things, and life is found in relationships.</u> We were made to live with one other, work with one another, and love one another.

We also believe that the core of our fulfilment in life comes from having good relationships on two fronts: firstly, with our Creator and secondly, with our fellow human beings. Jesus affirmed this in Mark 12:28-34. It reads:

> One of the teachers of the law came and heard them debating. Noticing that Jesus had given them a good answer, he asked him, 'Of all the commandments, which is the most important?'
>
> 'The most important one,' answered Jesus, 'is this: "Hear, O Israel, the Lord our God, the Lord is one. Love the Lord your God with all your heart and with all your soul and

with all your mind and with all your strength." The second is this: "Love your neighbour as yourself." There is no commandment greater than these."

'Well said, teacher,' the man replied. 'You are right in saying that God is one and there is no other but him. To love him with all your heart, with all your understanding and with all your strength, and to love your neighbour as yourself is more important than all burnt offerings and sacrifices.'

When Jesus saw that he had answered wisely, he said to him, 'You are not far from the kingdom of God.' And from then on no one dared ask him any more questions.

The lawyer's response puts a fantastic seal on Jesus's words when he says, "To love him (God) with all your heart, with all your understanding and with all your strength, and to love your neighbour as yourself is more important than all burnt offerings and sacrifices." In the eyes of God, the most important venture in life is to have a thriving relationship with him and a thriving relationship with people.

There is a reason why loving God is at the foreground. It is because a cordial relationship with God our Creator sets us up for fruitful relationships with fellow human beings. The Scriptures even affirm that a love for God is manifested in loving people. We read in 1 John 4:20-21:

Whoever claims to love God yet hates a brother or sister is a liar. For whoever does not love their brother and sister, whom they have seen, cannot love God, whom they have not seen. And he has given us this command; anyone who loves God must also love their brother and sister.

It is our hope that after reading this book, you will have the wisdom and necessary knowledge to propel your life in that direction. It is also our prayer that you will practise what you learn. In the words of Jesus Christ in John 13:17, "Now that you know these things, you will be blessed if you do them."

BEFORE WE BEGIN:
THE SEMANTICS OF COURTING AND DATING

The terms *dating* and *courting* have been used interchangeably throughout the 21st century such that the meanings seem uncertain at times when you mention them in public. You will find some people in the church who vilify the term *dating* as something ungodly. I have listened to the arguments over and over and I often find that we waste a lot of time arguing over things instead of defining them. When things are properly defined, we often realize we are in the same boat and stop fighting one another.

The crux of our belief concerning premarital relationships is this: a relationship between a man and a woman should not be a trial ground but rather a commitment heading to marriage. We believe that the idea of getting into a relationship for fun or "just to see where it goes" is a waste of time and the reason for so many emotional heartbreaks among many young adults.

What the world calls dating is often trial and error relationships with no commitment. In fact, the original use of the word *dating* came about in the early 1900s in America. There was a cultural shift from men pursuing women in the context of their families to pursuing them in the context of exclusive meetings in restaurants and entertainment joints. The modern version of dating has evolved in some social circles to often refer to a hook-up culture – no commitment to the marriage institution, just having fun. However, in many other contexts it retains a bit of the 1900s American model whilst combining the intentional pursuit of marriage.

For our context, we will use the terms *dating* and *courting* to demonstrate a chronological difference in the relationships between men and women. We will not use it to one-up each other theologically. *Dating* will refer to the period before an official request from the man's end to marry the girl. We will refer to *courting* as the period after that but before marriage. We will still use the term *dating* in this book because it is the culturally understood term for the kinds of relationships we are teaching. We hope the semantics will not result in unnecessary war of words that will only ruin those who listen. The Bible says in 2 Timothy 2:14, "Keep reminding God's people of these things. Warn them before God against quarrelling about words; it is of no value, and only ruins those who listen."

The use of the term dating in this book does not nullify the biblical viewpoint of man-woman relationships; it only helps us demarcate the timelines of the people in the relationship. The man-woman relationships we refer to are exclusive (meaning that the persons in them are faithful and committed to relating to each other as a couple and to each other alone). In light of that, we beseech you, our fellow fundamental brethren, let's not make a mountain out of a molehill.

1

FIRST THINGS FIRST

**YOU CAN HAVE A 100 PER CENT
CHANCE OF SUCCESS IN MARRIAGE
IF YOU DO IT GOD'S WAY.
JIMMY EVANS[1]**

The woman watched as the man on the ground lay sound asleep. She wanted to touch him, but she feared arousing him from his slumber. She did not want to scare him. She watched his bare chest rise and fall steadily as he inhaled and exhaled in his sleep. She took in his full form lying on the ground peacefully and imagined herself lying next to him. She imagined curling next to his equally naked form and resting in his arms until he awoke and found her next to him. Would he approve of her?

She ran her tender hands through her dark hair that dropped like a black waterfall onto her shoulders. She gathered it all in one tail and tied it in a knot behind the nape of her neck. Perhaps he may like her hair looking shorter like his, she imagined. She sauntered around his sleeping body, studying him and remarking to herself what a magnificent creature he was.

The sun came up in the hills in the distance. The shadows fled as light poured into the forest garden. She suddenly forgot all about the man and craned her neck at the winsome rise of the sun in the bright orange sky. She saw a flock of winged creatures fly in her direction, several feet in the air. The rays of golden sunlight pursued the flying critters all the way into a nearby cave above the waterfall. Her almond skin radiated in the sunlight. She basked in its warmth and took in the mesmerising sight of the sunrise.

She was almost lost in its enchantment until she heard him cough. She gasped and whirled. Had he awakened? Should she wait behind one of the trees, then reveal herself? She knew she was conspicuous in the greenery of the forest garden. He would not miss spotting her. She resumed her position behind him and began to look for a place to wait. She thought it out again and opted to stay put.

She hoped he would be pleased at her vulnerable sight. She hoped he would like what he saw. The wait unnerved her. Her cheeks grew hot, and her breathing pace increased. What was this feeling in her body?

The man didn't move, though. She took a few steps closer to him and her body's reactions multiplied in intensity. She stopped. He was making her breathless already. She rubbed her bare arms when a chill swept past her. She imagined it was the wind out in the open, though she heavily doubted it. The temperature was perfect. The chill was caused by her tension.

She looked at the man and she knew that she was breathless with desire for him. She longed to hear him speak. Was his voice like hers? His build was definitely different. He was sturdy and hard; she was soft and curved. She admired his build, but she liked her own. She looked up and waited for a sign. Maybe Elohim would give her direction. Nothing came.

Why did she have to meet him like this? What would he say when he saw her? Why wasn't he waking up? Would it not be terribly awkward if she startled him?

Adam awoke quietly. He had dreamed of heaven. The images in his mind were hazy and he couldn't exactly describe how heaven was. His eyes peeled open and came in contact with a clear sky, flooded with fresh sun rays. He arose slowly from the grassy lawn where he had fallen asleep and immediately felt the change in his body. His right hand swept up to the left side of his torso. He felt the skin closing in. He jerked his palm away and shot his face to the opening on his side. A healing scar was taking nature's course. Some blood was on the grass. He feared he might have slept on a sharp stick or stone. His left hand searched the ground around his sleeping spot. There was nothing. What had caused him to bleed?

Then he felt her presence. Even without seeing her, he knew someone was in the vicinity. He was used to Elohim's surprises. Without turning, he spoke aloud.

"So have you come again to indulge me on how vast the universe is or are you still expanding it?"

The woman heard him speak and had no idea what he was talking about. She parted her lips to speak but nothing came out. What would she say? Was this part of the introduction?

"So, it's the silent treatment, huh?" Adam asked. Elohim didn't respond.

Adam turned slowly to face the Creator. Contrary to his expectation, Elohim wasn't the one standing behind him. He jerked backward, a little surprised, when he saw the woman. Adam rubbed his eyes. There before him in full sight was the most alluring sight in all of Eden. Surely Venus had landed on Earth. Adam's eyes scouted the work of beauty standing mere feet away from him. This creature was very familiar and enchanting. Why he couldn't shift his gaze from her, only heaven knew. She was he, only a bit different. She was unlike anything he had seen, yet like everything and more than he had desired to ever behold. He knew who she was the moment he took in her breathtaking sight – she was his.

Adam erupted in a fit of infectious laughter. His eyes lit with excitement! He laughed with so much exuberance, he feared she may deem him mad like the monkeys.

"Yes! Yes!" he cried out.

The woman's heart skipped at his deep baritone. His reaction elicited a lot of interest in her. They were alike yet so different. She watched him leap in the air and cry out again.

"Yes, yes!"

A smile colonized her lips and she too erupted in laughter!

"Oh Lord, she is beautiful! She is beautiful!" Adam cried out. He looked up at the sky and cried again, "She is beautiful, Elohim!"

Elohim. That word was known to the woman. At least she understood that part of his talk. The woman stood immobilized, a smile pasted on her face, her shoulders shaking slightly with light laughter. She blushed when he studied her. His eyes hardly blinked. She was taken aback by the man's stare towards her but grew soft when he calmed down.

"My name . . . is Adam. What's yours?"

It was strange. She thought about it. She did not know. She was about to speak when suddenly she was up in the air. He grabbed her in his arms and swung her around. The woman giggled in delight. The man was very strong. She rested, shelled in his embrace, as he sank to his knees holding her and muttering words to Elohim. She heard him whisper in a deep heartfelt voice.

"Thank you! She is beautiful!" Then in calmness he said, "This is now bone of my bone and flesh of my flesh. Your name shall be woman," Adam said. He felt the scar on his side with his right hand. "*Woman* means out of man."

At the mention of that name, the woman blushed. Her blood coursed through her body in passion. She loved that he liked what he saw. She looked deep into his eyes and saw that he felt the same as she. She saw passion, desire, and she saw a future.

Elohim descended from the sky in a bright light that flooded the forest garden. Adam presented the woman before the great white light that stood before them. The woman stood by Adam, speechless at all that was happening.

"With your permission," Adam said to the light.

"Go forth!" a voice emerged from the light.

Adam went down on both knees, grabbed the woman's palms, looked up into her sparkling eyes and said, "Dear woman, will you be my spouse?"

The woman giggled, looked at the light that she recognized as Elohim, looked back at the giddy man, and said, "Yes!"

And there in the morning of the garden, the man and his woman were united by Elohim. The first proposal. The first wedding. The first marriage. They were both naked and they felt no shame.

START WITH GOD

The story above is simply my own imagination and should not be used for theological teaching; it should simply be taken at face value as fiction. That is how I imagine Adam and Eve had their first encounter. It was the world's first romantic relationship, and it didn't need several co-producers, assistant directors, make-up artists, and stunt men to execute it. It was a successful love story because it had one person at the centre of it all – God.

If we want to get the basics of marrying well right, we must start with the beginning of everything – the Creator God.

Genesis 1:1 begins by saying, "In the beginning God." If these first four words of Genesis are true (and they are), then it would only make sense to admit that all of God's creation works well under his instruction and authority. And it is not an assumption. Throughout the Bible, God emphasizes this.

When he is out of the picture in money matters, enslaving debt, greed, covetousness, and avarice strike. When he is out of the picture in relationship matters, envy, adultery, hurt, and all kinds of relational dysfunction strike. If you want to marry well, you must have a God-centred life, or if you like, a theocentric life. Anyone seeking to know how relationships with the opposite sex ought to thrive should start here. Most people reading that imagine that I'm saying you ought to go to church and be religious. Far be it! I need you to go to the start of human history and see what I mean. The first four words of Scripture are "In the beginning, God." These words are more than the opening sentence of the Bible. They reveal the main character. They reveal who the story is about. They demonstrate who has the spotlight. And if you fail to see that, all you need to do is read all the canonized 66 books of Scripture. God's Word is about him. Life is about him. He is in the spotlight of the entire production.

For many people, the spotlights of their lives have themselves at the centre. As opposed to a theocentric life, a humanistic one is adopted. A humanistic life is all about self; one's goals, one's ambitions, one's place in the universe and one's own happiness. Perhaps even picking this book was a means to get yourself more in the spotlight. Genesis 1:1 implicitly asks us to surrender the spotlight to the one who deserves it. We are not the chief protagonists; God is. And if the God of the Bible does not have this place in our lives, then every effort to enjoy any of his gifts, including that of a romantic relationship with the opposite sex will be futile. It will be the classic cart before the horse.

When you recall the encounter we just read of Adam and Eve, you may be tempted to take it at face value as merely the love story of Adam and Eve. God is challenging us to see this love story as the result of lives in which he holds the right place. That kind of romance develops when each party in the relationship lives life theocentrically. A blazing romantic union is a fringe benefit of a relationship where God has taken the position of sovereign Lord.

Unfortunately, for a majority of people in our world, romance has taken centre stage. It has become the main act and God has been reduced to a filler performance during the break. He has been denied the centrality he deserves and has been relegated to the role of an advisor and consultant when the romance is dwindling. Some people only run to God when their act is falling apart. And they hope he will take the role of a stunt man and fix their mess when they pray. And if he doesn't, they may challenge him with pseudo-threats such as, "If you are truly a good God . . . " or "If you really care for me . . . "

But, you see, such statements ultimately find their root in the belief that we are life's main act. They are humanistic in nature and not theocentric. If you think so, you may believe that God exists to fund your life campaign with his blessings. And if you live like that, most of your good deeds will ultimately be directed to yourself – bribes to God to use his superpowers to keep you at the centre and in control. But the God of the Bible is telling us that he is not an assistant; he is God. He is the main act and we are his creation. And his gift of relationships with the opposite sex will only be realized to the maximum when we accept that he is God and we are not.

We will get a glimpse of Eden in our relationships when we pursue the giver of Eden and not Eden itself. To want a great relationship with the opposite sex while wanting nothing to do with the Creator is not uncommon in our generation. Looking to creation to give you what only the Creator can give you is the first error in our pursuit of romantic relationships. If you want to get the basics of marrying well, you must realize that God is not a means to our happiness; rather, our happiness is a result of God being in charge of our lives.

C. S. Lewis states: "God cannot give us a happiness and peace apart from Himself, because it is not there. There is no such thing."[2] So, do you want marriage more than God? You should want God more than marriage. Do you want anything more than God? You must want God more than anything.

IF YOU WANT TO MARRY WELL, YOU MUST HAVE A GOD-CENTRED LIFE.

But the Bible teaches us that none of us innately wants God more than anything. Romans 3:10-12 says, "There is no one righteous, not even one; there is no one who understands; there is no one who seeks God. All have turned away, they have together become worthless; there is no one who does good, not even one." This is a serious claim the Bible makes. All our goodness is being nullified by the one from the beginning – the only good one – the only God. Nullified on what grounds? On the grounds of sin – our sin. Romans 3:23 says, "for all have sinned and fall short of the glory of God." What is sin? The original term for sin stems from an analogy of an archer missing the target of a bullseye. The bowstring twangs. The arrow is fired. But it misses the target. The target is God's standard of righteousness. And every human being has missed and is always missing the target. All have sinned. All fall short. All miss the mark. Even the Pope, Mother Teresa, and

Billy Graham combined offer no close shot to God's standard. But sin not only becomes a misfired shot. It becomes a way of living. We are slanted to sin. We are predisposed to miss the target. Psalm 51:5 says, "Surely I was sinful at birth, sinful from the time my mother conceived me." We are all born with this defect. And with this defect comes no desire to please God but rather to please self.

We have no desire to be theocentric; all within us screams humanism. The primary motive of sin is to keep us focused on self and place God at the sidelines, if not get rid of him altogether. Timothy Keller once said, "We are so instinctively and profoundly self-centred that we don't believe we are."[3] A man cheating on his wife is not merely him breaking the vows he made on his wedding day; he is placing himself selfishly at the centre stage of life and kicking God out. His desires matter at that moment and nobody is stopping him. A woman bent to sleep with someone's husband is placing herself at the centre of the universe. Her wants become king at the moment and no Bible will tell her otherwise. And this is just the extreme stuff. The lying, the fornication, the bitterness, the gossip – all that ruins relationships on a daily basis is simply because God's position of being in charge of how life should run is being challenged by a selfish human being.

And because God's gift of freedom to express the will is available to every human being, the hurt can escalate to global catastrophes such as terrorism, rape, and murder. God is not to blame. Every human being that abhors God's standard is. The terrorist and the cheating spouse have far more in common than they think: they all detest a theocentric way of living. The fornicator and the rapist have far more in common than they believe; the former detests a theocentric view of waiting for sex until marriage while the latter detests a theocentric view of consensual sex. Their actions may bear different consequences but their rebellion to God is similar and it is sin.

Sin inside of us does not want God to take his rightful position in our lives. And it is for that reason that in our fallen sinful state, we generally disdain his standards on sex, money, relationships and virtually anything that he has to talk about in his Word – the Bible. Human beings in their sin have no pure desire to wait for sex until marriage, to pray for their enemies, to think of others better than them and to keep all the Ten Commandments. And if they think we do, God is clear to let us know that those good deeds are filthy rags to him (Isaiah 64:6). Even our most righteous deeds are infected with sin's selfishness. We often give to the poor when there's an audience to see us – it's not about them but about us. The outside may be a white-washed tomb, but the inside is a rotting carcass.

You may have possibly picked up this book and said, "Just give me the tips on having a great romantic relationship without any of the mumbo jumbo about God." We believe that is a dangerous thing to ask. It is synonymous to asking the pilot to get you airborne and then have him take a parachute and leave the rest of the flight to you. If you are not trained to fly, you will crash that plane. You need the pilot in the plane if you want to enjoy the flight and if you want to arrive alive. You need the pilot not just in the plane, but in the right place in the plane – the cockpit.

But even if you believe in God and stand for a theocentric way of living, you still need this. Even believers often kick God out of the picture. There is a word for that; the Bible calls it *idolatry*. From our experience in mentoring believers, God is still on the plane, but he has been given a passenger seat. You need the right person in the cockpit and that person cannot be you. That can only be the Creator.

IDOLS AND THE HEART

I just mentioned that the insubordination of rejecting a theocentric life is called idolatry. It applies to your relationships. If you insist on having a relationship with the opposite sex without having God at the centre of your life, you will fall into the crushing disappointment of idolatry. Idolatry is substituting anything else for God. An idol is a God-substitute. It is the thing that you look up to; the thing that is the source of your life's significance, security, and sense of being loved and accepted. It is the thing that is your refuge in times of trouble, anxiety, worry, and doubt. It is what gives your life meaning. It is what you run to when your world is falling apart. Idols may be money, power, human approval, sex, one's good looks, one's moral standing, or even a person.

And when we don't have a theocentric way of living, our hearts become easily magnetic to idols. The trouble with idols is that they take the role of God and vow to fulfil what he can, but they fall drastically short in delivering their promises. Idols in themselves are often good things. The bad thing lies in what we ask of them. We often ask idols to substitute for God and give us what only he can give. Well, what is it? What is this that only God can offer? What is the thing that gives us a theocentric life? The answer is the gospel. The gospel is the only way to live a theocentric life. From the gospel, we learn that God gives us what our hearts deeply long for. And what our hearts deeply long for is unfailing love, assured security, and purposeful significance. And from these three things we can understand what the gospel is, what our hearts long for, and how God offers it.

UNFAILING LOVE

When a boyfriend forgets his girlfriend's birthday and a fight breaks out, a few things may be said by either party which are unloving. They may even end the relationship on that note. The boyfriend failed the girlfriend. When the girlfriend disrespects her boyfriend in public, a verbal fight might ensue. Things may get ugly and embarrassing. The girlfriend failed the boyfriend. Often in a relationship, we know we are loved based on the response we receive from our partner. If you were asked, "How do you know you are loved by your partner?" you will most likely respond by stating how they react to your goodness towards them. The love we receive from them is often based on our current behaviour and actions. It is conditional. And when this current behaviour and actions fail, the couple often states, "We have fallen out of love."

God's love is different. God offers unfailing love. What does that mean? Well, for starters it means that his love is without conditions attached. His love for you does not change based on your behaviour, the lack of it or our circumstances. Human affection tends to do that. Unfailing means that it is unconditional. It is not altered by good days and bad days. It is constant. Secondly, it means that it is flawless. It is not seamed with underhanded demands. And God demonstrated this love for you perfectly in the gospel through the person of Jesus Christ. This flawless and unconditional love was demonstrated in the mission of Christ on Earth. His goal was to pay for the sins we committed. To do that he had to offer himself without expecting any favour from us because we are incapable of offering anything of significant value to a holy God. Knowing we could offer nothing, he came anyway. This is unconditional love. To be accepted by God, he had to live without sinning. And this he did. This is flawless love.

The Bible teaches us that his death was a substitutionary punishment. Take it as if this life is an exam. None of us can pass the exam of life because we all fall short of God's glory. Christ Jesus our Lord decided to sit the same exam of life that we failed and he passed 100 per cent. But here is the game changer. He took his paper and erased his name and wrote yours instead. He took your failed exam and erased your name and wrote his. His perfect score of 100 per cent is now credited to you and your failures are debited from him. You receive eternal life for an exam you never participated in if you accept Christ.

And what does Christ get? Thirty-nine lashes of the whip. A split-open back bleeding like a tap. A crown of thorns piercing his veins. Scorn and abuse. He hangs naked in front of his mother and followers. He is pierced on the side and mocked to come down and save himself. Yet his hanging on that cross is saving us. The wages of sin is death and Jesus took the tab. You are accepted into God's Kingdom, not because of anything you have done, but simply by believing on him who did it all for you. It will take humility to admit you cannot sit the exam and see how much he loved you.

Christ's flawless and unconditional love is the water that our sinful hearts long for. His love says that we are affectionately embraced and our sin is taken away, even when we have failed completely. And his flawless record is now imputed on us and we are perceived by God as if we never sinned. The abortion is forgiven. The lies are forgiven. The adultery and fornication are forgiven. The words we could not take back are forgiven. All is forgiven for those that ask. 1 John 1:9 says, "If we confess our sins, he is faithful and just and will forgive us our sins and purify us from all unrighteousness."

Jesus Christ never failed you. He took the punishment of flogging and crucifixion you should have taken. He never failed you. He lives a flawless life on your behalf. He never failed you. He then laid his life down and rose from the grave. He never failed you. Christ will return for those that are his. And if you belong to him, he promises he will never fail you. His love is unfailing.

The only source of unfailing love comes from the cross of Christ – the gospel. We see God pour out unconditional affection towards us by sacrificing his only Son. And if we can grasp the gospel, we can realize that it is futile to expect this kind of love that our souls crave from any other source. Any other source that claims to offer this is an idol. Any other thing that competes with God for your heart in this regard is an idol. I once saw a funny meme on Facebook that said, "Ladies, this man Jesus died for you; your boyfriend cannot even faint for you." Behind the humour is a deep message that unfailing love is found in the one who died for us to rescue us from mortal death. This is the deep-set longing of your soul, and your boyfriend or girlfriend cannot give it to you.

ASSURED SECURITY

God offers assured security. The second deep longing for the human soul is to be secure. On a base level, we prefer secure neighbourhoods, we lock our doors, and we insure our cars. Why? We want everything to remain intact when storms come. Our deep longing for security is revealed in times of trouble. And whatever we run to is our source of security. The most common thing humans run to for security is money. Look at what Job says:

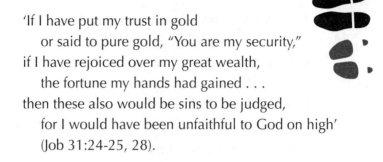

'If I have put my trust in gold
  or said to pure gold, "You are my security,"
if I have rejoiced over my great wealth,
  the fortune my hands had gained . . .
then these also would be sins to be judged,
  for I would have been unfaithful to God on high'
  (Job 31:24-25, 28).

Job considers hoping in finances for security to be unfaithfulness to God. He implies subtly that God should take that role of security in his life. The futility of Job's money as security is seen when it is incapable of saving him from the calamity he faced. A 100-dollar bill could neither stop the Titanic from sinking nor preserve the life of any man on board. For you who hope to marry well, you must know that money is not the only idol of security that is wooing your heart.

Your security may also be in a person. When we find ourselves defaulting to a human's view above the Scriptures, we have left a theocentric life and placed our security in mere mortals. When we run to men and women to help escape the worries, troubles, doubts, and anxieties of this world, we have placed our security in mere mortals. Yet humans are so feeble. Human relationships face the uncertainty of people failing us. Even solid marriages face the uncertainty of death. Then what happens when your security lies in a coffin and is being lowered six feet under?

The gospel says that the most secure place you can be is in having your sins forgiven and being eternally saved from the punishment of your sins. The gospel says that the biggest security for your soul is in having a relationship with him. And God in his compassion for you guarantees a safety zone.

The Lord is compassionate and gracious,
　　slow to anger, abounding in love.
He will not always accuse,
　　nor will he harbour his anger forever;
he does not treat us as our sins deserve
　　or repay us according to our iniquities.
For as high as the heavens are above the earth,
　　so great is his love for those who fear him;
as far as the east is from the west,
　　so far has he removed our transgressions from us.

As a father has compassion on his children,
　　so the Lord has compassion on those who fear him;
for he knows how we are formed,
　　he remembers that we are dust
　　(Psalm 103:8-14).

Look at that! God understands your weakness and stands by you. He doesn't reject you, cast you aside, and give up on you. And he assures us that if we rest in his love through the gospel of Jesus, we will not be separate from him.

For I am convinced that neither death nor life, neither angels nor demons, neither the present nor the future, nor any powers, neither height nor depth, nor anything else in all creation, will be able to separate us from the love of God that is in Christ Jesus our Lord (Romans 8:38-39).

Our safety is so solid and everlasting that God promises security that surpasses the certainty of death. Any other source of security for your soul is an idol and with it is a crushing disappointment when it fails to deliver.

SIGNIFICANCE

God offers significance. The third and final deep longing for your soul is to have a life worth living. With the certainty of God's love and security for your life, the natural response for those that submit to him is to live for him. When God's love and security for your life is unsure, the natural response is to try to look for something else to live for. For some it could be a career, children, or even a marriage. But these things only become idols because they cannot quench the deep desire of our soul. Only the gospel can. The gospel says that as soon as you submit to Jesus for the forgiveness of your sins, he gives you prime status at that moment.

He begins by calling you his friend: "I no longer call you servants, because a servant does not know his master's business. Instead, I have called you friends, for everything that I learned from my Father I have made known to you" (John 15:15). The Creator of the heavens is not calling you a servant but a friend.

He continues by calling you his child. John 1:12 says, "Yet to all who did receive him, to those who believed in his name, he gave the right to become children of God." On account of your sin you were an enemy of God. Through his gospel, the enmity is dissolved. Your status is no longer inimical to him. You are restored to a position of sonship. You are family. The murderers of his Son have been invited to be his children.

He then bestows power and authority to you. Romans 8:17 says, "Now if we are children, then we are heirs – heirs of God and co-heirs with Christ, if indeed we share in his sufferings in order that we may also share in his glory." God then states that through his gospel you have ruling power similar to Christ. This shall be manifested in the millennial Kingdom when all evil will be destroyed, but we must realize that the author of

Romans does not use future tense. He says "you are", not "you will be". The God of the gospel is giving you a power that no earthly source can guarantee.

Why would the God of the gospel call you a friend, his child, and grant you all this undeserved power? Apart from the overarching reason of his passionate love, it is also because he has work for you to do. He requires your life to reflect his character. He requires you to live for him and bring many who do not understand the gospel into his sheepfold. When we live for anything else more than we do for the God of the gospel, we devalue our purpose. When a man tells a woman that he lives for her, it sounds romantic, but it is cheap. When living for the God of the gospel, all other areas in your life fall into place (including a romantic relationship with the opposite sex).

WHEN A MAN TELLS A WOMAN THAT HE LIVES FOR HER, IT SOUNDS ROMANTIC, BUT IT IS CHEAP.

THE GOSPEL AND YOUR IDENTITY

David said this about false gods or idols: "Those who run after other gods will suffer more and more. I will not pour out libations of blood to such gods or take up their names on my lips" (Psalm 16:4). David is right – when the place of God is taken by a person, we suffer more and more. Idols promise you unfailing love, assured security, and purposeful significance and require you to sacrifice to them in order to get them. Yet they don't deliver at all. David must have found out about that the hard way and was inspired to write this verse in Psalm 16. He stopped sacrificing to false gods that don't satisfy. Jesus is the only true God who does not require your sacrifice to fulfil you.

On the contrary he sacrificed himself on the cross to demonstrate that you are loved, secure, and significant if you believe in him. Bruce Marshall stated, "The young man who rings the bell at the brothel is unconsciously looking for God."[4] When anything else (even a person) takes the place of God, it is a reflection on your identity.

Whatever makes you know you are loved, secure, and significant feeds your identity. God requires that your identity is in him before you come into a relationship with the opposite sex. Imagine you were called for dinner by the president – just you. The president wanted to meet you only! Imagine him sending a chopper to pick you up with six bodyguards. But after the dinner, you would be back to your old self. No plane. No bodyguards. No State House. Earthly love, security, and significance do not last. But God's love does.

IDOLS AND RELATIONSHIPS

So before we look at the basics to marrying well, we must ensure that the foundation we are building on is rock solid. We must start with God. Two of our favourite marriage speakers are Jimmy and Karen Evans. Pastor Jimmy frequently says, "You can have a 100 per cent chance of success in marriage if you do it God's way." Are you doing it God's way? Is he Lord? Have you uprooted the idols of your heart? Have you started with God? You must deal with the idols in your heart as far as relationships are concerned in order to marry well. Here are a few questions that can help us confirm idolatry.

Have my current/past relationships interfered with my personal devotion to God? Have relationships with the opposite sex interfered with my proximity to the God of the gospel?

Have these relationships been spiritually draining yet have me still cling to them powerfully? For a believer, have your current/ past relationships hindered Christian fellowship? Have they cut you off from fellowship of the Word with other believers?

Does the absence of the relationship cause anger or inconsolable frustration? Does the idea of not being married/ not being with this person debilitate us and leave us joyless? Does the idea of this relationship ending give me deep-set anxiety, worry, and even depression?

Without this relationship, is my life without real, lasting meaning? Do I get my sense of importance and reputation from having a relationship with the opposite sex? If your relationship was to end, would you conclude that you are ruined? Does the idea of being single sound like a curse?

Do I depend on this relationship for my spiritual growth? Is it the core support of my life? Do I rely on this relationship to meet my financial needs or to maintain emotional stability?

The alternative to idolising marriage is idolising independence, which I have not belaboured. However, Keller states: "While traditional societies tend to make an idol out of marriage (because they make an idol out of the family and tribe), contemporary societies tend to make an idol out of independence (because they make an idol out of individual choice and happiness)."[5] The most common result for those who idolize marriage is to compromise on convictions. The most common result for those who idolize independence is to become impossible to please as far as selecting a mate and settling down is concerned. The God of the gospel must take centre stage in our hearts in order for us not to fall victim to any of these false gods. If we truly want to marry well, we must start with God.

2

YOU NEED A MASTER

**YOU ARE UNDERQUALIFIED FOR THE JOB OF MASTER
AND COMMANDER OF YOUR OWN LIFE.
TIMOTHY KELLER[6]**

A friend of ours broke up with his girlfriend. A few weeks later, he was telling us of this new girl he had met in church and wanted to start dating. When we suggested that he take things slow and evaluate his previous relationship, the man said that he just couldn't imagine himself single. Besides, he said, what if the girl was taken by someone else while he was in his singlehood? Would he ever get another girl like her? This fear was causing him to jump into a new relationship with a girl he hardly knew barely three weeks after the previous break-up. The relationship that had ended had lasted for over two years. He neither took time to evaluate the relationship nor to mourn the loss.

Do you see the problem here? The man perceives singlehood as a problem. In his own words he admitted, "I can't stay single." Unfortunately, many young adults view singlehood in a similar fashion. Yet the single years are actually a fantastic time to prepare for a relationship. Once our identity and foundation are anchored in the gospel and once we realize that the only way to be truly fulfilled is to live a theocentric life, then we are ready to take the right step in the direction of relationships. And that step is not finding a boyfriend or girlfriend. That step is thriving in your singlehood.

Singlehood is not a curse. It is a blessed time to explore yourself and do so much in preparation for a dating relationship. The Bible gives us a great picture of the first single man that ever existed – his name was Adam. Adam came before Eve. Then Adam met Eve. We can draw a few lessons about how to thrive in our singlehood by studying single Adam in Genesis.

A SINGLE PERSON IS FUNCTIONAL AS AN INDIVIDUAL

> The Lord God took the man and put him in the Garden of Eden to work it and take care of it (Genesis 2:15).

In Genesis 2 we see that the creation of Adam as a human being was a complete job. Before the woman is added to his company, Adam has a life to live with God-given responsibilities. God does not put his life on hold as he waits for Eve to come into the picture. Your singlehood is not merely a transit point to a relationship. It is a thriving point for your individual life.

Before Eve comes into the scene, we can see three things to be true of single Adam. We can see that he has a Master, he has a mission, and he needs a mate. This is the Master-mission-mate model by Ken Graves in his guide for Christian singles. Before we look at it, I must state that this is not a formula for getting married; it is a guide. Some people think that they can use this as a formula to get rewarded by God for doing all the right things. This is a guide for those who understand the need to place priorities in life.

Religion operates on the premise that if I obey, I get rewarded. Ken Graves's model is based in the gospel that states you are already accepted by God, therefore obey. A religious heart feels that God owes it a mate. A gospel-changed heart knows that God owes it nothing and if anything, it owes God everything; obeying the Lord becomes a joy not a duty. The latter understands that we don't *have to* worship God but rather we *get to* worship God – privilege not pressure. Have this at the back of your mind as we tackle the Master-mission-mate model. Ken Graves puts it like this:

YOUR SINGLEHOOD IS NOT MERELY A TRANSIT POINT TO A RELATIONSHIP. IT IS A THRIVING POINT FOR YOUR INDIVIDUAL LIFE.

> Ideally, here's how it should work. You come to God. You make Him your Lord and your King – your Master. You accept the invitation to take up your cross and follow him. And the longer the walk behind him and with him, the more you begin to understand how he views you, how he feels about you.
>
> If the Lord Jesus Christ is your Master, then he will determine your mission. At some point, as you draw closer to him, he begins to reveal to you the plan He's laid out for your life. Part of that mission includes being conformed into His image, into His likeness, but there's another part that is unique to you. The Lord will direct you to that thing you're intended to do with your life. He'll open your eyes to the things you've been gifted to do and help you navigate the choices you'll make about your occupation and how you might serve him vocationally.

Then – and only then – you begin to seek a mate who can help you fulfil that purpose. It's vital that you have some understanding of who you are before you go out looking for someone to match up with you. If you don't know who you are, you're not going to have any clue who you're looking for, or at least who you're hoping for. That's not so hard, is it?[7]

MASTER: WHO IS YOUR KING?

Adam understood clearly that he was created by God. He knew that God was the Alpha and the Omega. It is upon this understanding that he is even able to execute the commands he receives concerning taking care of Eden. He realizes he is a steward with a master. Adam's understanding of his origin is characterized by having a relationship with God. Only in having a relationship with God will Adam understand his Master. He will know his voice. Single persons ought to cultivate their walk with God so deeply that it defines who they are – their identity. This way, someone of the opposite sex, no matter how breathtaking, will not dissuade them from their devotion to their Creator. Any relationship that pulls you away from God is a distraction. As a single person, ask yourself: do you know your Master?

Everyone who invests to understand their origin will also not be swayed and disarmed by circumstantial pain in life. They will accept all as filtered by the Creator and appreciate the common treasures that fellow humans easily take for granted, including a romantic relationship with the opposite sex. Are you in a personal relationship with your Creator? Are you conscious of your origin? God is a holy God and humanity is sinful. Because of sin we cannot know our Master. However, God bridged this gap by having his Son, Jesus, die on the cross for the sins of humanity. Because of that, a personal relationship with God is possible.

Knowing our Master like Adam knew his is a reality. A relationship with God through his Son Jesus is imperative, because he is our origin. The world wants good relationships but does not want God. To divorce God from the relationship process is suicide. We came from God. We will return to God. The biggest asset you can bring into a relationship as a single person is a thriving walk with God through Christ.

Some people at this point may think that having God as their Master simply means believing that he exists. That's the worst mistake you can make about this. Psalm 14:1a says, "The fool says in his heart, 'There is no God.'" When we see this verse, we immediately think of atheists who say there is no God. We even claim to see the foolishness in their denial of a God. The complexity of the human body, the change in weather seasons, the beauty of nature and so many things paint the picture of a supreme being who made it all happen. If it's an accident then it's a pretty detailed, accurate, and intelligent accident. But we know we are more than an accident.

But perhaps Psalm 14:1 is not just referring to intellectually saying there is no God. Perhaps this verse also has moral weight for the one who believes in a God. There are people who believe that God exists, but they live their lives like he doesn't exist. And I believe they too qualify to be called fools. Psalm 14 says, "in his heart". So these are people whose beliefs are within them.

Surprisingly, just like atheists, there are theists who may hold this belief when it comes to their moral life. The prayer of the atheist on his deathbed may be, "If there is a God, please save my soul, if I have one." But the theist knows there is a God, knows that he or she has a soul, but at times lives in the opposite. When we refuse to surrender our money to God, we become financial atheists and for that we are fools. When we refuse to submit our sexuality to God, we become sexual atheists and for that we are fools. Psalm 14:1 is a challenge not just to believe in God but to surrender as well. For God to be your Master, you must surrender to him fully. He must be your King! He must be Lord of all or he is not Lord at all!

The deeper problem is that the single person doesn't trust the Master like Adam did. And the dominant reason is that marriage has been made to look like a contract and not a covenant. A contract has termination options and is based on performance of the other party. A covenant has relational considerations and is based on serving the other party. A contract requires the other party to sustain an act or else ship out. A covenant requires one to put up with the other party and help her or him grow. A contract is between formal partners. A covenant is between friends. Formal partners ask, "What's in it for me?" Friends ask, "How can I serve you?" A contract has individual needs prioritized above corporate needs. A covenant has mutual needs prioritized above individual needs. A contract has "either/or" options. A covenant has "both/and" options. A contract doesn't have much regard if the other party has relations affected by it. A covenant realizes marriage has more involvement than two people who are simply in love. Covenants honour family. Contracts honour self.

The world's first concern is, "What if I get burnt in this relationship? I need to take care and place security measures." God's people's first concern is, "How do I take care of this person who is God's gift to me?" The world says alarms are put up to protect the house from burglars. God says a human being is a person and not a house and you cannot treat a subject as you would an object. We fear we will miss out if we do things

God's way. We fear having Christ as a Master because of three main reasons.

1. We think that God is not benevolent.
2. We want control.
3. We don't understand the gospel.

1. WE THINK THAT GOD IS NOT BENEVOLENT

The first reason we don't trust Jesus as our Master is because we think his plans are out to harm us. It is a lie from hell. When I was single, there resided in me a sinful thought that God would send me to a remote tribe in West Africa to live a difficult and horrible life as a missionary if I surrendered to him as Adam did. It is a fear that the Monarch we give the throne to is a dictator. That God is a tyrant who will not get us a husband or a wife, so we "liberate" ourselves to have sex lest we miss out. That God is a tyrant who wants us to die poor, so my money is my money and mine alone. In all this, we doubt the benevolence of Jesus on the throne.

But you need to realize that if Christ was that dictator who pushes his will down our throats, he would have done it a long time ago. Dictators do not wait patiently to be accorded their respect; they take it. Christ does not force his way on anyone. Dictators don't allow themselves to be placed on the sidelines; they conquer their way to the throne. Yet, the conquest of Christ is through benevolence. As the famous Napoleon Bonaparte once said:

> I know men, and I tell you that Jesus Christ is not a man. Superficial minds see a resemblance between Christ and the founders of empires and the gods of other religions. That resemblance does not exist . . . Alexander, Caesar,

Charlemagne, and myself have founded empires. But upon what did we rest the creations of our genius? Upon force. Jesus Christ alone founded his empire upon love; and at this hour millions of men would die for him.[8]

If a man of war could sense the benevolence of Christ, why would we doubt it? Single man or woman, submit to Jesus fully. Let him write the story and discover that his plans are for good and not for evil (Jeremiah 29:11).

2. WE WANT CONTROL

The second reason we don't trust Jesus as our Master is because we don't want to relinquish control of our lives. In Matthew 11, we see Jesus speak about those that do not trust him and surrender to him. When Jesus spoke of the towns that refused to believe in him, he noted that their unbelief wasn't rooted in a lack of evidence. He preached to Bethsaida, Chorazin, and Capernaum and did many miracles but they did not believe in him. Even though Christ overwhelms an unbelieving people with miracles and wonders, they fail to believe. Why? He gives an analogy of children playing out in the street. They start by playing a dancing game, but the children refuse to dance. They then change the tune and play a dirge for funerals, but the children refuse to cry. They don't want to play either game. It is not because they don't understand the tune, but it is simply because they want to play the pipe. They want to be in control of the game. We are like the towns of Bethsaida, Chorazin, and Capernaum; our problem with trusting Christ is because we do not want to relinquish control of our lives, our plans, and our comfort.

I can tell you this: For the many times I have put Jesus on the bench, the lessons have been painful and hard. And the root of my desire for control is pride. Christ becomes a consultant and an advisor and ceases to be a Saviour. And like every proud heart, disaster is just a matter of time. Do you think you know better concerning your sexuality, your money, and your relationships? If so, you have a huge wall of pride that will only come down with the sledgehammers of confession and humility.

The Creator knows the creation better than anyone else. I have also surrendered to the Lordship of Christ severally and I could tell you lots of stories of how the best parts of my life have come out of them. The single believer who desires it must be willing to lose control and leave it to Christ. It is a scary thought to lose control. However, if I've learnt anything, when you lose your life, only then do you find it. Surrender is a good thing. Surrender today. As Timothy Keller once tweeted, "You are underqualified for the job of master and commander of your own life."

3. WE DON'T UNDERSTAND THE GOSPEL

The third reason we don't trust Jesus as our Master is because we don't understand the gospel. It was once bizarre, but now very common to hear, "Get born again and Jesus will get you a husband." Or "Get born again and you will heal very quickly from your break-up." Or "Get saved and God will take away all your marriage problems." Present-day Christendom has been filled with a barter-trade gospel message that suggests God is trading his unlimited riches for all our circumstantial pain. We bow, he gives. He gives, we bow. It has reduced God to a vending machine where we insert the coin of pain and expect God to release the candy of blessings.

Postmodernists are now coming to a realization that this is not the God of the Bible. And if he is the God of the Bible, postmodernists have concluded that the vending machine is broken (God is dead). Some even believe that God owes us for the pain we experience on this earth.

PRESENT-DAY CHRISTENDOM HAS BEEN FILLED WITH A BARTER-TRADE GOSPEL MESSAGE THAT SUGGESTS GOD IS TRADING HIS UNLIMITED RICHES FOR ALL OUR CIRCUMSTANTIAL PAIN.

Single postmodernists who believe that sound like this, "I am giving God one more chance, then I'm done." Or "God had his chance, now it's my way." In short, they say that either God's arm is too short to save, or his ears are too dulled with wax to hear. While I am cognisant of the role of painful moments in bringing people close to God, I have to point out that the gospel of salvation has been greatly misunderstood by many postmodernists.

You can look around and see for yourself. When a friend decided to "take the Jesus thing seriously," he or she was asked what went wrong. Did your relationship end that badly? What was so bad that you needed God's help? To pop culture, salvation is a fail-safe to deal with those troublesome areas that you can't handle on your own. For them, God is the big butler in the sky for those that do things the churchy way. Or in short, it is what I call the barter-trade gospel. What they don't know is that nothing could be further from Jesus's plan for mankind's salvation.

The salvation of Jesus has bigger things to offer than the wife you want, the husband you desire, or the money you need. Don't get me wrong. Money, a husband, a wife, and all those things are good things – even in God's eyes. God wants them for us. However, when those things become the core of our existence, a huge problem develops. They become idols. When good things become ultimate things, they become idols.

Meredith MacInnis, a Facebook friend of mine from Canada, commented on one of my Facebook posts. In her comment she said, "We all have this longing for solid and healthy marriages deep down because we are made in the image of God, and he wants that for us." Her statement struck me. How profound! How true! The yearn for good marriages comes from our design – the image of God. And since that is true, it only makes sense that the ultimate love doctor is God Almighty. If we get God, we get his blessings as well. But to want God's blessings without wanting God is a tragedy. We must be careful not to be like the crowd in John 6.

In John 6, the crowd follows Jesus because they want the miracles and the food that he was giving. Jesus knows that they don't want his teaching, his Word or anything to do with eternity; they only want food. In fact, they even try to make him a king when he multiplies the food for them. In truth, they don't want him as their king; they want him as their butler who will multiply five loaves and two fish whenever they are hungry. They want his stuff not his presence. Jesus flees from them and refuses their kingship offer. Why? When Jesus is King, he doesn't just want the title, he wants the crown and the throne too.

In John 6, Jesus offers the people eternal life (the bread of life), but the people are only concerned about physical bread to eat for their stomachs. The focus of the crowd was the hunger pain in their stomachs, and it came in the way of God's salvation. Did Jesus care about the hunger pain? If he didn't care, would he have fed them with the five loaves and two fish to start with? He does care; however, he will not allow himself to keep being King over people's short-term needs if it hinders them from experiencing long-term, eternal benefits. Jesus is not a friend with benefits. He is not a utilitarian deity. He is a Saviour! He is a King! The question is: Is he your Saviour and King? To anyone that desires to marry well, Jesus must be Master. Run hard after God; if anyone catches up, introduce yourself.

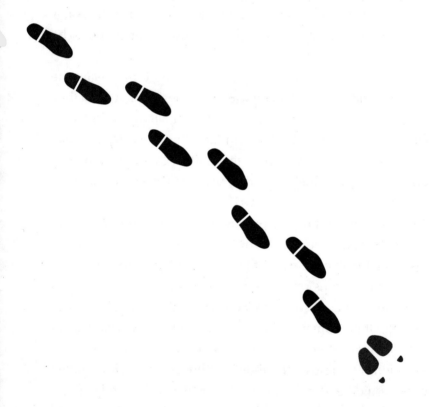

3

YOU NEED A PURPOSE

**THE LORD GOD TOOK THE MAN AND PUT HIM IN THE GARDEN OF EDEN TO WORK IT AND TAKE CARE OF IT.
GENESIS 2:15**

In this Scripture, we see that Adam has work to do. We must remember that he is still single. He is commanded by God to tend the garden and watch over it. Adam had a purpose that was to be fulfilled through working. Every single person should be working and fulfilling their God-given purpose as they wait for a lifetime relationship with the opposite sex. God knows your need for a relationship even before you realize. This can be proved by looking at Genesis 2:18-22.

The Lord God said, 'It is not good for the man to be alone. I will make a helper suitable for him.'

Now the Lord God had formed out of the ground all the wild animals and all the birds in the sky. He brought them to the man to see what he would name them; and whatever the man called each living creature, that was its name. So the man gave names to all the livestock, the birds in the sky and all the wild animals.

But for Adam no suitable helper was found. So the Lord God caused the man to fall into a deep sleep; and while he was sleeping, he took one of the man's ribs and then closed up the place with flesh. Then the Lord God made a woman from the rib he had taken out of the man, and he brought her to the man.

The Lord conceives Adam's need for Eve and what does he do? Send him to an online dating site? No! He gives him more purpose. He burdens him with more purpose. He was told to tend the garden. Now he is told to name the animals. After Adam named the animals, he was on course to receive Eve. Only when Adam was on board with God's mission for him was he nearing the possibility of a lifetime with the woman of his dreams. We can imagine that the animal naming made him realize that there was an issue. There was Mr. and Mrs. Hippo, Mr. and Mrs. Elephant but no Mr. and Mrs. Adam. God orchestrates for Eve to come into Adam's life at the peak of Adam's pursuit of God's command. And so we ask you, single person, are you on your Master's mission?

DON'T DO SOMETHING ABOUT YOUR SINGLEHOOD; DO SOMETHING WITH IT

A postmodern tragedy of our time among single people is not only not having God as their Master but also living an empty and purposeless life. In our ministry we see a number of people just waiting to get married! They are so anxious – as if it is a train they will miss if they don't position themselves well. The idols of the culture tell men to be financial gods; they conversely tell women to be sexual goddesses. So the guys show off lifestyles they can't afford. The ladies expose body parts to get some male attention.

PEOPLE ARE PREOCCUPIED WITH DOING SOMETHING ABOUT THEIR SINGLEHOOD INSTEAD OF DOING SOMETHING WITH IT.

They get onto multiple dating sites. They attend every party they are invited to. And they almost get depressed when things are not working out. All these people are preoccupied with doing something about their singlehood instead of doing something with it. It's a bad move. Each person will give an account to God for their lives. What has God placed you on Earth to do?

Men especially need to know that purpose is one of the things that arouses a woman. A man pursuing a purpose will always win the heart of a woman. Beyond that, the thing that keeps your marriage fuelled is spiritual mission. God does not bring a man and a woman together to simply get married, make babies, pay taxes, and then die. There is a mission that your future marriage will be called to. And focusing on that mission will keep your future marriage from petty squabbles.

I often see in my own marriage that when we deviate from the spiritual mission God has called us to, our fights become petty. The man must realize that he is the vision bearer in the marriage. He should not wait to marry to seek this vision. He must invite his woman to an adventure by seeking it earnestly before he walks down the aisle. He may not have a full idea of what it looks like, but he should know the general direction.

But women should not just be seated on the sidelines looking pretty and waiting for a man with a purpose. God has made us in his image, both men and women. There is purpose for the woman to pursue, as well, as a single person. A woman on the path of purpose discovery will know the kind of man she is looking for because their purposes will align. A man or woman devoid of purpose will always fail to launch and constantly give excuses for why a task was never done. They will keep wandering in a miasma of peer pressure, constantly bowing down to the demands of the latest trends – including getting into a premature relationship.

Persons of purpose are steadfast. They may not have everything together, but they are headed in a godly direction. Purpose is not about perfection, but about vision and direction. We believe that Adam qualified for a mate because he went on God's mission. A lack of purpose disqualifies you from enjoying the beginning of a great relationship with the opposite sex.

WHAT DOES PURPOSE/MISSION LOOK LIKE?

I believe purpose is twofold for the believer. Firstly, purpose is specific. Secondly, purpose is universal. Let us look at each.

Specific Purpose

One way to do go about discovering your purpose is to prayerfully search the SHAPE acronym from Pastor Rick Warren.[9] SHAPE stands for: Spiritual gifts, Heart, Abilities, Personality, Experiences.

What are your spiritual gifts? Are you fanning them into flame? Where do you exercise them? How is God using your gifts to bring his Kingdom on Earth as it is in heaven?

What is your heart? What are the passions that you have? What are the themes in life that capture your heart? What problems in our world do you feel led to solve?

What are your abilities? These are either acquired abilities or natural talents. What's on your skill list? How can you use your skills and abilities to expand God's Kingdom on Earth?

What is your personality? This is a crucial area to your purpose. You must understand that God custom-made you for the task ahead of you. The field of psychology has given us truths from God that can help us understand why we behave the way we do. I recommend *www.16personalities.com* to start the personality discovery.

What are your experiences? Your experiences may lead you down a certain path. It is how Joseph got into his purpose. He was sold as a slave to Egypt. That was an experience. He was framed for rape and thrown into prison. That's an experience. He was elevated to Prime Minister. That was an experience. All these experiences (good and bad) later led him to admit that God was working in the background to lead him to his purpose. He even tells his brothers that their act was meant for evil, but God used it for good (Genesis 50:20). And that good was to fulfil the purpose God had for him; to save lives.

Universal Purpose

Secondly, purpose is universal based on the command of Jesus. He put it clearly for us in Matthew 28:18-20:

> Then Jesus came to them and said, 'All authority in heaven and on earth has been given to me. Therefore go and make disciples of all nations, baptising them in the name of the Father and of the Son and of the Holy Spirit, and teaching them to obey everything I have commanded you. And surely I am with you always, to the very end of the age.'

Notice that Jesus begins by saying that all authority is his. This is before he commissions them. He is talking to his disciples. There is an assumption that Jesus is their Master. Master comes before the mission. Then he dishes out the mission. What is the mission? To make disciples! To walk with new converts and bring them to maturity. To do exactly what Jesus did with the Twelve. To live like Christ, by the power of the Holy Spirit. Therefore master the Master's life. What is the mission, you ask? The mission is to master the Master's life and replicate it in the lives of others! That's what a single believer (as any other believer) ought to be preoccupied about as he or she anticipates a romantic relationship with the opposite sex.

Are you doing this? There is work to do! Adam was fulfilling his master's mission. Are you, like Adam, about God's mission in your singlehood? Ladies, are you discipling and walking with a group of younger ladies? Gentlemen, are you discipling and walking with younger men? My wife and I believe that every believer should pour out their life and the truths of Scripture to those younger than they are or new in the faith. We believe that discipleship is the best pursuit of purpose. Discipleship is not a 10-week course done in a church. Discipleship is a lifelong journey. It is frustrating, tiresome, and very slow but the rewards are out of this world (literally).

Getting married does not stop us from pursuing this purpose either. I disciple a group of men that I meet with every fortnight on Thursdays. My wife disciples a group of young ladies every fortnight on Saturdays. The ladies meet at our house for breakfast twice a month. Together, we disciple a group of couples pursuing marriage. The single person should be about God's business and God will be about the single person's business, just as he was with Adam.

Hindrances

But what hinders us from pursuing the mission God has called us to? Here are five hindrances:

1. We don't invest in our purpose.
2. We have made marriage an end goal.
3. We don't understand the gravity of the mission God calls us to.
4. We are obsessed with building our own empires.
5. We don't see the gospel as Christ in mission.

1. We Don't Invest in Our Purpose

One reason we don't pursue the mission of God is that we don't invest in the purpose God has called us to. In fact, we often pursue pleasure and not purpose. I get amazed at how many people in our generation can sit for six hours straight watching a television series. While relaxation is important, we must be honest with ourselves when the television series viewing is several hours a day almost every day. There are gifts and abilities that God has put in us waiting to be unearthed.

But how can I perfect my guitar skills when I am not even committed to practice? How can I begin that blog when I cannot commit to reading? When will I start my 10,000 hours? Christ needed only three years on Earth to fulfil his mission because he invested

WE OFTEN PURSUE PLEASURE AND NOT PURPOSE.

well. We have a generation that is not burning to ask, "What has God called me to do?" You must realize that when you are burning with passion on a mission, you want to spend the rest of your life with someone who is accelerated in the same direction. Many young people are interested in purpose but are not necessarily committed to it. If we were committed to it, we would invest in it.

2. We Have Made Marriage an End Goal

A second reason we don't pursue the mission of God is that we have made marriage an end goal. Inasmuch as we desire marriage, we must recognize that it is not the ultimate goal in life. Marriage is a good and noble union that men and women should pursue. In fact, it is one of the few things that shares a characteristic with God – hence we say "holy matrimony." Hebrews 13:4 says that marriage ought to bear the respect and esteem of all, especially sexually.

But we must remember it is not an ultimate. However, the ultimate goal in life still takes the form of a marriage – just not the earthly one. It is the heavenly one between Christ and his bride. If our earthly marriages came with job descriptions from God, one of them would be "to reflect the heavenly marriage". A husband loving his wife demonstrates the love God has for humanity. A wife submitting to her husband demonstrates the loyalty the church has for her groom. But when the aisle is glorified above Calvary, we will hit a snag even if we had the honeymoon of a lifetime. Upon the foundation of Jesus is a good marriage built, but away from the direction of Jesus is a good marriage split. An earthly marriage is finite, but the heavenly union is infinite! The earthly marriage lies to waste on the arms of death. The heavenly marriage was forged in the arms of death. Even the first perfect marriage between Adam and Eve points us to the heavenly marriage. Adam was pierced on the side of his rib to create his bride. Similarly, the last Adam, Jesus Christ, was pierced on the side of his rib to create his bride, the church. Adam sunk into deep sleep and awoke to his bride, Eve. Similarly, Jesus Christ sunk into the sleep of death and awoke to his bride, the church. Our ultimate goal is not to hear the words "I do" but rather to hear the words "Well done, good and faithful servant!"

We see marriage as a destination instead of seeing it as the start of a journey. We have made marriage a finish line instead of seeing it as a mission field. Our generation seems to love weddings more than marriages. And because we don't see marriage as a mission, we invest more in the flowers of the wedding than the premarital counselling. You get married. Then what? God doesn't just call us to get married, have kids, then die. Nay! He asks that our marriages be set on fire on a mission to demonstrate the gospel.

Our ultimate life reward is not "I do" but "well done". The latter can be propelled by the former. Ephesians 5:24-25 says "Now as the church submits to Christ, so also wives should submit to their husbands in everything. Husbands, love your wives, just as Christ loved the church and gave himself up for her." A thriving marriage between a man and a woman submitted to God is one of the most vivid signs of the gospel of Jesus.

This should be the goal of every newlywed couple in the church. We should even place these words in the vows of believers: "I promise to make the gospel the mission of our marriage." If you do not see marriage as a mission, you will settle for anyone. God wants you to realize that choosing the love of your life should not be on the basis of eye candy but on the basis of soul food.

3. We Don't Understand the Gravity of the Mission

A third reason we don't pursue the mission of God is that we don't understand the gravity of the mission we are assigned. When Abraham met God in Genesis 17:1, he turned into a man on a mission. When Moses met God in Exodus 3, he turned into a man on a mission. When Isaiah met God in Isaiah 6, he went into mission. He cried out, "Here am I. Send me!" The

Scriptures are freckled with so many examples of people who encounter God and go into mission. Some left everything to follow God. They understood that the mission was important. A genuine encounter with God will translate into mission. Mission at your school. Mission at your work. Mission in your business.

Mission is the inevitable result of meeting God. And it is a big deal because he is inviting you to partner with him for the salvation of human souls. This means letting Christ be seen in the work he has called us to do by doing it well. As the famous quote states, "The Christian shoemaker does his duty not by putting little crosses on the shoes, but by making good shoes."

The world ought to marvel at Christ in you and desire it. That's mission. And it is very important because, ultimately, the souls of men are at stake. It is also important because God wants to reclaim this world to its Eden state. You and I are his agents. Mission was the last call of Jesus before he left. It should be our first priority. Jesus went up; the Holy Spirit came down; you should go out.

4. We Are Obsessed with Building Our Own Empires

A fourth reason we don't pursue the mission of God is that we are preoccupied with building our own empires. All human empires will ultimately be castles in the sand. When we live to make a name for ourselves instead of making an impact in this world for the Lord, we can get carried off in the love of money, the deceitfulness of wealth, and the cares of this world. And if we get there, we can be sure we will attract the wrong mates.

I get many people who ask me, "Ernest, how come I attract the wrong people?" I tell them to get on the right mission track. Only people who care for the things of God will stick to its path. It will repel all the wrong ones. Start a date by saying "no sex until marriage" and just see how many people will run off the path. Our mission should focus us on the Maker and not ourselves. We ought to fix our eyes on Jesus in our singlehood as we do his will.

If you understand that the Kingdom of God is infinitely larger than all the multi-billion-dollar companies on Earth, you will realize that it is important to marry someone who cares about advancing the gospel more than advancing their career. If you understand the gravity of the mission, you will realize that it is important to marry someone who cares about winning souls more than winning arguments.

If you understand that God's will is more important than our feelings, you will realize that it is important to marry someone who cares about being a good witness of the gospel more than being a good lawyer of his sins. If you understand true success, you will realize that it is important to marry someone who cares about the return of Christ more than the returns of her hard work. And God is eagerly waiting to reward those that participate in his Kingdom mission.

5. We Don't See the Gospel as Christ in Mission

The final reason we don't pursue the mission of God is that we have taken our eyes off the gospel. We don't see Christ engaged in a mission. His death has become cliché for many. Christ came to Earth and began a restoration process that seemed impossible since Genesis 3. His mission on Earth resulted in his death and it ended the spiritual singlehood we were in. He laid down his life for us. That sacrifice should compel us to do anything for him. He proposed to us when he died on that cross. If we accept him, we join an eternal spiritual marriage. I pray we never lose sight of Christ in mission.

A faithful God gave Christ his bride while in mission. A faithful God can do the same for us in our singlehood. In conclusion, we must realize that in a marriage, mutual spiritual mission is a core pillar. God's desire for you is not simply to get married, have sex, have kids, pay taxes, then die. His desire is for each Christian marriage to reflect the love of Christ and the church. One ought not to think about this only after marriage. It should be meditated on in one's singlehood. It will help you in the selection process. You will not merely look for an attractive member of the opposite sex; you will look for a life partner to achieve God's mission here on Earth as it is in heaven.

4

YOU NEED TO WAIT

IF GOD COULD GET ADAM A MATE IN A WORLD WITH NO HUMAN BEINGS, HE CAN DEFINITELY GET YOU ONE IN A WORLD WITH SEVEN BILLION.

When I asked Turi to marry me, I had no idea I would find myself seated in the middle of a wide circle of chairs with her father, grandfather, uncles, and older cousins. I had proposed to their daughter and they wanted to know if I meant it! They asked me several questions that could be summed up in this one: "Why do you want to marry our daughter?" I was growing weary of answering it. Still, I recited my response with a positive face. It had been three hours in the same chair surrounded by about 10 men who were sceptical that a college graduate knew anything about settling down with a woman. I sat in the middle of their council as I was hard-pressed to answer question after question. I was doing my best to convince her male family members that I was serious about my relationship with her.

I look back at that moment and I really appreciate it. Yes, you heard right. I appreciate it. I thank God for Turi's father who didn't make it easy as pie for me to get his daughter. I thank God for the uncles and grandfather who grilled me with questions concerning my background, my finances, my faith, and my family. Not because any of these things were perfect but because they mattered when it came to where they were taking a family member of theirs. I also thank God because that back-breaking experience made me a better husband. One of the men in the grilling session tested me by telling me that I was free to date other women and compare them to Turi. They would keep Turi for me. If I didn't like those other women, I could always come back. I respectfully declined. Perhaps you have faced a similar or harder time in getting a mate. But I posit that Adam had a harder time. As we keep reading the Genesis account, we notice that Adam is in need of a mate, but he is the only human being on Earth.

So the man gave names to all the livestock, the birds in the sky and all the wild animals.

But for Adam no suitable helper was found. So the Lord God caused the man to fall into a deep sleep; and while he was sleeping, he took one of the man's ribs and then closed up the place with flesh. Then the Lord God made a woman from the rib he had taken out of the man, and he brought her to the man.

The man said,

'This is now bone of my bones
    and flesh of my flesh;
she shall be called "woman",
    for she was taken out of man.'

That is why a man leaves his father and mother and is united to his wife, and they become one flesh.

Adam and his wife were both naked, and they felt no shame (Genesis 2:20-25).

In verse 20, we see that Adam has named the animals. The Scriptures then say, "But for Adam no suitable helper was found." The contrast word *but* seems to imply that Adam noticed everyone in Eden was hitched except him. At this point, I believe Adam began to have the desire for a mate. This is the desire that God had in verse 18 when he said it is not good for man to be alone. It is important to note that God had this desire even before Adam did. Now Adam is aware of his need for a woman. But when he looks around there is nobody.

Let me encourage you. If you desire to be married but look around and see nobody, take heart and just wait on God. If God could get Adam a mate in a world with no human beings, he can definitely get you one in a world with seven billion. Do you desire a mate? We bet Adam did after naming those animals. But whose plan will you rejoice in? Yours or God's? Some Bible language experts say that when Adam saw Eve and cried out, it was in song. The language is poetic! And that's exactly what having a mate from God is – beautiful poetry! If you want a taste of heaven and a glimpse of God's love, look at a working marriage! And a working marriage is a result of rejoicing in God's will.

Do you trust the Master enough to lead you to the right person or are you afraid that God's will is bogus and outdated? We recently read an op-ed piece in a local city magazine. The writer claimed to be a practising Christian but blatantly called the Judeo-Christian sexual stances archaic. We were not surprised by this. Many people who claim to be in the faith are self-deceived. Paul implored us in 2 Corinthians 13:5 to examine ourselves and establish that we really belong to Christ.

Unfortunately, we are in a generation that believes since they go to church, sing the songs from the projector, take their children to Sunday school, and know the Bible stories, they must automatically be Christians. Religiously, they may be, but spiritually, they are still dead. A person who goes to church is no more a Christian than a cow that sits in a garage claiming to be a vehicle is a car. When self-proclaiming believers vehemently fight God's biblical stance, we can smell from a mile away that they do not rejoice in Christ but in themselves. God's will is the best thing that could ever happen to you because he knows the desires of our hearts and he fulfils them. I, on the other hand, think I know the best desires of my heart. But the Scriptures warn us about the heart in Jeremiah 17:9-10:

> The heart is deceitful above all things,
>> and beyond cure.
>> Who can understand it?

> 'I the Lord search the heart
>> and examine the mind,
> to reward each person according to their conduct,
>> according to what their deeds deserve.'

Let God be involved in your mate selection. Allow godly men and women who walk with God to be involved. If God gave me what I deserved, I would be dead. But since I allowed him to have his way, he gave me what I do not deserve. And one of the things I do not deserve is a lovely and humble wife like Turi. I want the same for you and even better.

IF GOD COULD GET ADAM A MATE IN A WORLD WITH NO HUMAN BEINGS, HE CAN DEFINITELY GET YOU ONE IN A WORLD WITH SEVEN BILLION.

Adam slept and his rib was taken out and Eve was fashioned for him. But what if Adam had been panicky and rebellious? Imagine for a moment that Adam, after naming the animals, realized he had no mate. He decides not to rejoice in God's plan and decides to venture out on a mate-finding mission. He grabs a vine and begins to swing through Eden like Tarzan looking for his Jane. God realizes that Adam is panicky about being single!

"Adam, I need to put you to sleep."

"No way, God. I need to find a mate for me. Everyone in this hood is in a relationship."

"Adam, just trust me and it will be okay."

"No way."

Many of us would be like that made-up version of Adam. Saying "No way" while all we need to do is trust Yahweh! And after much resistance, we can imagine Adam finally returns home after a hard day of working the garden and presents to God his mate.

"Here you go, Lord, I finally found her!"

God is lost for words!

"Adam, that's . . . um . . . a chimpanzee!"

"Yeah, a bit hairy but she'll do."

"But if you only trusted me . . . "

"Yeah, yeah, I know! But your plan was taking too long so I decided to help you!"

"But you two are not the same."

"Well, not entirely true, God. I mean, I think we have about a 99 per cent DNA match!"

Whenever we read the Scriptures and see someone try to help God, the result is always chaos. Sarah tried to help God by having Hagar sleep with Abraham. The result was Ishmael and a lot of political chaos. King Saul tried to help God by sacrificing on behalf of Samuel. The result was a lost kingdom and the death of his loved ones. Many people are not rejoicing in God and are trying to help God instead of trusting him. We must wait. Stop opening accounts on every dating site you find. Ladies, stop taking selfies on Facebook and Instagram to show that you're available. Men, stop worrying that your rib has been used to make some soup! Stop changing churches because the men and women there are hot. Instead, submit to God your Master, enrol in his mission, and trust him for a mate. But why don't we trust God's will for our mate? I will give you three reasons.

1. We think marriage's main goal is happiness.
2. We think we can change people.
3. We don't realize marriage is a big deal.

1. WE THINK MARRIAGE'S MAIN GOAL IS HAPPINESS

Waturi and I meet many young people who want to get married. We like that. We encourage them. But often when we ask, "Why do you want to get married?" they respond, "because I want to be happy." And we ask, "What if your marriage makes you unhappy on most days?" The bewilderment is clear on their faces. Why would we say that to them? We ask, "What if marriage is primarily not to make you happy but to make you holy? What if marriage is a refinement process for your character? What if happiness in marriage is a by-product of a refined husband and a refined wife? What if the way to stay happy in marriage is to submit to the refining process? What if marriage is not the goal in life as far as relationships are concerned? What if marriage is but a mirror of an ultimate heavenly marriage? What if this latter marriage is the ultimate life goal? What if our focus on the altar is meant to refine our focus on Calvary?"

Christ is not just a means to a better relationship with your spouse. Your spouse is also a means to a better relationship with Christ. One of the purposes of marriage for believers is to refine themselves and become more like Christ. Your marriage is not primarily to make you happy, but to make you holy and Christlike. And if you pursue the holiness, the happiness will automatically come. But if you pursue happiness and neglect holiness, you may just miss out on both.

God achieves a refinement of character through your marriage partner. If you are teachable, a godly marriage can make you humble. If you are not, even if you married the best spouse on Earth, your heart will be as hard as a rock with pride. All your flaws and worst sides are brought out in a marriage. When that happens, believers realize that they need to work on their relationship with Christ in order to be a better spouse. When that happens, they become more mature Christians (a good relationship with Christ) and they become a better husband or wife (a good relationship with the spouse).

2. WE THINK WE CAN CHANGE PEOPLE

If there is a hopeless pursuit among the young people of our generation it is trying to change people. And this false thinking causes many not to trust God. People hope to date chimps that will turn into Adams and Eves. We hear people say, "I will date them to change them." Not only is it a futile attempt, it is also a very proud one. An attempt to change people is to innately believe yourself better than those people. At times what we are not saying is louder than what we are

PEOPLE ARE NOT PROJECTS.

actually saying. People who compromise their faith in an attempt to change other people simply show they do not value their faith. Or even scarier, they may not genuinely be in the faith. People are not projects. The attempt to change people is often masked by our claim to love the other person. But in a true sense, it is because we love ourselves; it is selfishness. We want our will to be done at the expense of the other person. I call us out to have enough self-integrity to know when a relationship is not meant to work out and trust God's bidding. Because at the end of the day, there are only two kinds of people:

- Those who say to God, "Your will be done!"
- Those to whom God says, "Your will be done."

What blessedness it is to have God's will in your life and what horror it is for God to give you up to your own paths. As Romans 12:2 puts it, his will is a good, pleasing, and perfect will!

3. WE DON'T REALIZE MARRIAGE IS A BIG DEAL

A third reason why we don't trust God's will for our mate is because we don't value marriage as God does. I have heard people equate marriage to a college degree or a football game. I have also heard single people trash it as if it's a man-made thing. But we must realize that marriage is a big deal for a number of reasons.

First of all, marriage in Hebrews 13:4 is termed as holy. "Marriage should be honoured by all, and the marriage bed kept pure, for God will judge the adulterer and all the sexually immoral." That's why we call it holy matrimony. I am not surprised that many people would bad-mouth marriage, yet it is holy. Hebrews 13:4 explicitly commands us to honour marriage – that means even in our speech.

Humans have a knack for messing with holy things. The name of Jesus is holy and yet people trash it when they use it as an expletive or a cuss word. God's Word is holy yet humanity pokes fun at it. If you read your Old Testament, you realize that anything holy, if defiled, invited the wrath of God. God's grace right now gives us room to repent. At his second return, he is not coming as a baby in a manger; he is coming as a king of wrath and glory. May we not be found in dissonance with what he calls holy matrimony.

Secondly, marriage is a big deal for society. Gary Chapman asserts that in every human society, without exception, marriage between a man and a woman has been the central social building block of that community.10 An assault on marriage is an assault on community.

Thirdly, marriage is a big deal for you. It matters whom you marry because before you say "I do" you may have the freedom to choose your love, but afterwards, your only option is to love your choice.

Fourthly, marriage is a big deal for the gospel. Marriage is so powerful in God's economy. It is the only relationship that existed before sin came into the world. It was the only relationship that tasted a perfect life. Adam and Eve expressed love emotionally, rationally, physically, sexually, and spiritually without the interference of sin. God wants us to experience Eden. But we can't until we understand why marriage is so important to him. We can't rejoice in his will like Adam did until we understand the potency of marriage. Marriage is powerful in God's economy because it is the relationship analogy that he uses when he describes his relationship with us, the one he loves. Look at all these Scriptures that allude to that:

God as our husband:

> For your Maker is your husband –
>> the Lord Almighty is his name –
>> the Holy One of Israel is your Redeemer;
>>> he is called the God of all the earth (Isaiah 54:5).

Israel as God's passionate and devoted bride:

> Go and proclaim in the hearing of Jerusalem:

> 'This is what the Lord says:

>> "I remember the devotion of your youth,
>>> how as a bride you loved me
>> and followed me through the wilderness,
>>> through a land not sown"' (Jeremiah 2:2).

Israel as an unfaithful spouse to God:

> 'But like a woman unfaithful to her husband,
>> so you, Israel, have been unfaithful to me,'
>>> declares the Lord (Jeremiah 3:20).

God as a scorned husband:

> 'Rebuke your mother, rebuke her,
>> for she is not my wife,
>> and I am not her husband.
> Let her remove the adulterous look from her face
>> and the unfaithfulness from between her breasts'
>> (Hosea 2:2).

Jesus as the bridegroom:

> Jesus answered, 'How can the guests of the bridegroom
> mourn while he is with them? The time will come when the

bridegroom will be taken from them; then they will fast'
(Matthew 9:15).

John the Baptist as God's best man:

> To this John replied, 'A person can receive only what is
> given them from heaven. You yourselves can testify that I
> said, "I am not the Messiah but am sent ahead of him." The
> bride belongs to the bridegroom. The friend who attends the
> bridegroom waits and listens for him, and is full of joy when
> he hears the bridegroom's voice. That joy is mine, and it is
> now complete' (John 3:27-29).

The church as a virgin in waiting for her husband:

> I am jealous for you with a godly jealousy. I promised you
> to one husband, to Christ, so that I might present you as a
> pure virgin to him (2 Corinthians 11:2).

Eternity as a wedding:

> Let us rejoice and be glad
> and give him glory!
> For the wedding of the Lamb has come,
> and his bride has made herself ready
> (Revelation 19:7).

Perhaps the most compelling of Scriptures that affirms God's
relationship with us as likened to a marriage is from Ephesians
5:24-25. It says:

> Now as the church submits to Christ, so also wives should
> submit to their husbands in everything.

Husbands, love your wives, just as Christ loved the church and gave himself up for her.

Marriage is not in league with any other relationship. It is uniquely powerful. A thriving marriage between a man and a woman submitted to God is one of the most vivid signs of the gospel of Jesus. The world is attracted to it. When Turi and I are not walking right with God, the marriage suffers. And for the seriousness of it, as you transit from singlehood to having a partner, do not initiate a relationship with the opposite sex if you do not aim for this serious marriage. This is counter-cultural! Our pop culture says you can date for fun. We say, if you date for fun, you could break up for fun and it won't be funny! Know your Master passionately. Pursue his mission radically and you will find your mate graciously! May God's favour be upon all who obey, till death do you part.

5

BE THE ONE

WOULD YOU MARRY YOU?

Almost every young person hopeful for marriage that we meet has a list. They want someone who loves children, who prays and walks with God, eats healthy, is understanding, is kind, is sensitive, etc. We often ask them: "Are you even half of those things that you want?" Too many young people are spending lots of time, money, and emotional energy looking for "the one" instead of becoming "the one". It is troubling for the marriage market – if there is such a thing! Everybody is seeking for a service that no one is offering. Are you the person whom the one you are looking for is looking for? Or, in other words, would you marry you?

BE THE ONE: WOULD YOU MARRY YOU?

I interact with people after I'm done preaching or teaching, and I hear them say that they want to marry prayer warriors that wake up at 3:00 a.m. and pull down the strongholds of the enemy. And I ask them, "What about you? Do you wake up to pray at 3 a.m.? Do you pursue that quality you like with similar passion?" They shrug their shoulders and say to me, "That's why I need a strong person in that area because I'm weak." And my question begs, "Why leverage on your weakness when you can work on it?" That person you want to marry may be your strength, but you will be their burden! I must give a disclaimer that most of these people are sincere lads and lasses. But I must also give a fair verdict that they are sincerely wrong. At times I must mind my own business and at times I am compelled to intervene.

"What makes you think that the kind of person you want to settle with, wants to marry someone their opposite in virtue?" You want to marry a spiritual ninja, but you are okay with being an alternate version of Homer Simpson? Hard words to swallow but come on! How can you expect to find the one when you are not "being the one"? It's like shopping for a new television in the grocery section! Don't act surprised when all you get is tons of unripe mangoes instead of HDMI technology. In order to be the one, you must understand this first principle: You can only attract someone who pursues the same depth as your pursuit.

So the most important question for a single person hoping to get married is not "What kind of person do you want to marry?" but rather, "What are you pursuing?" What is your pursuit and how deep are you into it? My wife and I always say that if you want a godly spouse, then pursue God with all your heart and be that godly spouse. Only pursue a relationship with someone who is pursuing God as ardently as you are.

BE THE ONE: REALIZE IT'S NOT "MEANT TO BE"

Another way to become the one is to get rid of dangerous pop culture themes you may have believed that destroy relationships. One common pop culture theme goes like this: "Our relationship is meant to be!" This idea of relationships *meant to be* assumes that there are pre-made people who will be as compatible as Lego pieces once they meet. It assumes these people are ready for each other. It assumes these people are intact and don't need to work on a few things. It discounts the idea that people are sinful. It also discounts the truth that there are seasons when you shouldn't be looking for a life partner. The season of thriving in your singlehood is such an example. When you are fresh out of a painful break-up is another. Wisdom dictates that such seasons be handled without pursuing a life partner. But pop culture ideologies such as *meant to be* can trump that wisdom when you meet the "person of your dreams" two days after a nasty break-up. Tim Keller puts it like this:

> It is possible to feel you are "madly in love" with someone, when it is really just an attraction to someone who can meet your needs and address the insecurities and doubts you have about yourself. In that kind of relationship, you will demand and control rather than serve and give.[11]

When we focus on finding the one and not becoming the one, we overlook our own insecurities and weaknesses. In fact, those very insecurities and weaknesses end up making us repeat the same mistakes we made in old relationships because we always imagine we are the victims of our exes. Being the one means realizing that you could be the villain in someone's story.

This takes humility and teachability. But if you simplistically believe that you were meant to be, you will only look at how this person met your list at the start of the relationship and how she or he doesn't meet it right now after the break-up.

The idea of *meant to be* also discounts the fact that you could marry the wrong person. "What does *meant to be* entail?" we often ask. Often when people say "meant to be", what follows is a job description of how stars should align, bad circumstances should turn around, and how God should wave a magic wand and make things work out for the person who is living contrary to all the clear warning signs from wisdom!

A young lady we met got into a relationship with someone who didn't value her biblical values on chastity and her devotion to Christ. Since she felt they were *meant to be* she persisted in her plan despite the best efforts by her spiritual overseers to convince her that dating the guy was not a wise move. But alas! They were *meant to be*! Who wants to argue with the forces of *meant to be*? She compromised her rectitude and the relationship began to quake. The same people with spiritual oversight advised her to break up with him. She was in a hole and she was told to stop digging. But she thought to herself, "How can I break up with him, yet we were *meant to be*?" Her train of thought kept digging the hole. She figured, "Since we are *meant to be,* getting married will make things better."

And so she pursued the agenda with colourful nuptials! Then the guy changed for the worse after they got married. She realized (a tad too late) that she had compromised and injured not only her walk with God but also with those friends closest to her who looked like enemies when they were looking out for her all along. She then asked us a befuddling question. "If God didn't want me to marry this person, why did he let me fall in love with him?" We then realized that this *meant to be* idea is a shifting goal post. It only works when things are going well. But it is conveniently ignored when things go wrong. And unfortunately, God becomes the target for one's poor decisions. When we enter relationships seeking to be served and not seeking to serve, we are likely to look for someone to blame when things go wrong. See what the Scriptures say in Proverbs 19:3, "A person's own folly leads to their ruin, yet their heart rages against the Lord."

We must not equate our faulty Hollywood idea of *meant to be* to God's endorsement of a relationship. That train of thought is from the brainwashing deception of our pop culture – that since it happened naturally it must have been from God. In short, it was *meant to be*. We can tell you for free that there are people out there who assault naturally and kill naturally but it isn't from God and it wasn't *meant to be*. And if that happens, what makes you think that when you make the natural wrong decision concerning a relationship, God had a hand in it?

The killer chose to dishonour the Lord and become a killer just as we choose to spend lots of time and conversation with the wrong persons and consequently fall in love with them. But we do feel a tad justified when we spiritualize our choices and lay the blame on the stars that did not align, the circumstances that did not work in our favour, and the God who did not wave the magic wand as he saw our hearts breaking. Part of being the one involves taking responsibility for your relationship choices and not placing the blame on God.

Our generation is scuba diving deep in this ideology and have forgotten what the surface world of reality looks like. Then they get married quickly because they were *meant to be* and the oxygen tanks run out of air and it is too far, too exhausting, and too late to swim to the surface to catch a breath from a newly troubling marriage. Before you said "I do" you may have had the freedom to choose your love but now, your only option is to love your choice. But you see the dire situation and create another choice – divorce. Too early. Too soon. And since the pain of staying in the relationship outweighs the commitment you didn't mean and understand, an early divorce is filed with the same reasoning that started the relationship. "Love didn't happen between us because it wasn't *meant to be.*"

BE THE ONE: SERVE

Alice wrote to my wife and me. She was frustrated with her husband. They had two children, a three-year-old and a one-year-old, and she was pregnant with their third. Her husband, Eric, would come home from work and sit on the couch and go online for two hours. She told him that those two hours were vital for her. She needed his help in the house. The babies needed to be fed and bathed. Dinner needed to be prepared. The dishes needed to be done. She needed to rest and unwind after a long day at work. Eric didn't budge.[12]

In his defence, he had a more demanding job and his evenings were his me-time. He did not understand. Since she got home an hour before him, why couldn't she do many of those things before he arrived? Alice argued that the time was not enough. Eric countered by asking why they have a house-help. To which Alice replied that the house-help only works in the day and leaves in the evening. They couldn't afford to have a stay-in house-help. Their combined income was not sufficient. Eric would then get into a frenzy stating they had to work with what they had. To Alice this meant that she had to just do what needed to be done and stop complaining. Alice began to grow resentful towards her husband. They talked less. They smiled less. They made love less. An invisible wall of indifference grew between them. Alice regretted having their third child. She saw this as added responsibilities without any help from her husband. When we met Alice, we asked her what she wanted.

"I just want him to treat me the way he did when we first got married."

"What do you mean?" we asked.

"At first he was so kind and supportive. We didn't have any children, but he would help around the house. He would do it for me. There are days he would ask me not to cook and we would eat out. I really felt like he cared for me. But now, all he does is go on Facebook and Instagram until his food is placed before him. And after that, he wants sex. After sex, he goes back to his phone and then retires for the night. Meanwhile I have to feed both babies, bathe the babies, tuck the babies to sleep, wash the dishes, neaten the house, and be up in time to do breakfast for us before our help arrives. I wish I had 15 minutes to sit and do nothing but enjoy a hot cup of tea. We don't even talk about our days. And I have grown resentful; I don't even want him to touch me. I only do it for him; I don't want some other woman out there to replace me."

I called Eric for a man-to-man meeting and asked him his side of the story. He didn't contradict Alice. But he insisted that his evenings are sacred resting times. "What makes you so tired during the day that you cannot help your wife with at least one of the chores?" I asked.

"Well for starters, my job. It's not physically tasking but it's mentally exhausting."

"Do you carry work to do at home?"

"No, I don't. It's not that tasking."

I challenged Eric to do something. During one of his leave days, he would switch house roles with his wife. For just one day while he was at home, he would carry out the chores his wife carries out. He was unwilling initially but for the sake of the marriage he consented. Eric had an experience that shook him. He only did half the chores delegated to him that day. He realized what his wife was saying. She must be Wonder Woman to have done all that she did. And to think that she did it every day made him feel shame because he remembered how often she asked for his help.

He realized that his sacred evening times were really selfish. Eric admitted how he had always thought he would be a different kind of husband. When he was dating Alice, he would consider himself someone who would be her knight in shining armour. But now he was married, and he seemed to be the dragon that imprisoned the damsel in distress. Eric admitted that he had taken his spouse for granted. He began to appreciate her whenever he found the house clean. Eric also found out that the social media and TV time did not make him relaxed; they made him more lethargic. He helped around the house more and the end result was a closer bond with his wife and with his children.

Eric's change and effort gave Alice some time to do some self-introspection. After Eric's improvement we asked her if she had some things to work on. On her own accord, she, too, admitted that she had taken Eric for granted.

"As we have been spending time in the evening bathing the kids together, I noticed I hadn't been there for my husband," she admitted. "He had been going through so much stress at work and I never asked him even once how his day was. He had no friend to talk to."

Alice continued to express how she realized that Eric could have easily gone to a bar after work or taken a detour instead of coming home directly. Instead, he came home faithfully every day. She had taken for granted the fact that Eric was physically available. The more she became grateful, the more her resentment faded. Coupled with Eric's new-found resolve to help her, their marriage experienced a renewal. Eric and Alice feared that they could easily slip back into ingratitude and taking each other for granted.

We encouraged them that the way out is not to look for the one in your partner but to be the one. And the way to do so is to serve one another. When you are preoccupied with meeting the needs of another, you hardly take them for granted. When it is mutual, it is a taste of heaven. Christ himself set an example for us when he came to Earth. Mark 10:45 says that Jesus came to serve and not to be served; he came to give his life as a ransom for us. Jesus demonstrates selflessness in his relationship with the church.

BE THE ONE: WORK

The other way to be the one is to realize that good relationships won't occur naturally; we have to work. The only natural thing after the start of a relationship is a break-up; everything else must be intentional. Relationships cannot take a natural course because we are sinful human beings. We are not naturally inclined towards good marriages. Our natural inclination is towards sin. See what the Lord says concerning our hearts. Jeremiah 17:9 says, "The heart is deceitful above all things and beyond cure. Who can understand it?"

Those who think we are naturally inclined to have good marriages see wedding vows in the same category as the decor – to create emotional effects and for the camera to capture. Those who know that we are naturally inclined to having horrible marriages realize that the vows are the most important part of the wedding even if you have no decor. Our marriage vows generically state that we will commit "for better and for worse, in riches and poverty, in sickness and health, with all our being, till death do us part". Why? Because the vows are being said by someone whose natural inclination is to do the opposite! Because being the one is maturing and realizing that relationships take work to start and even more work to maintain them. In the heat of temptation to break my vows, I realize that saying the vows doesn't make me capable; it only makes me accountable. Working at my marriage makes me more than capable to have sex with only one woman, be romantic with only one woman, and tell only one woman that she is beautiful. Everything about a relationship with the opposite sex must be intentional. And intentional is spelled W.O.R.K!

EVERYTHING ABOUT A RELATIONSHIP WITH THE OPPOSITE SEX MUST BE INTENTIONAL. AND INTENTIONAL IS SPELLED W.O.R.K!

One of the most deceptive trains of thought among a few young people is that "I can fool around now but when I get married, I will be serious and faithful in my relating with my then wife and other women." Loving faithfully and living honourably is not a superpower acquired by slipping a wedding band on your finger. A change of relationship status will not result in a change of heart. And that change of heart requires that we work to make our relationships work.

Consider this, when young men and women graduate from university with honours, do you think they attained that degree naturally? Nay! In fact, they poured in hours of sleepless nights, emptied cans of Nescafé, and lived in the library for days so that they could graduate with distinction. They gave it their all. Yet when it comes to the choice of a life partner, we somehow believe it will require less attention than acquiring our degrees?

I get amazed how men and women reject wisdom that would help them improve their relationships. Yet the same people will fight tooth and nail to get wisdom to save their careers. A certain married lady attended one of our marriage seminars alone. We asked her where her husband was. She told us his reason. He responded to her, "All those things they talk about in these conferences I can Google and find online." It's a reflection of our hearts. We assume relationships will work without work.

Another couple complained to us why their church charges to attend a 10-week premarital program.

"Well, is the program useful?" I asked.

"Of course it is. It has been recommended by so many people."

"And the church uses time, money, facilities, people, pays for your food and gives you marriage-saving truth and you are not willing to pay the price?" They went silent.

"Well . . . there are people who can't afford it," the lady said to justify their reason. "Are you one of those people?" I asked them. They went quiet. The reality is that we are often not willing to pay the price for successful relationships. Proverbs 4:7 says: "Get wisdom. Though it cost all you have, get understanding."

6

FIND THE ONE

How do we ensure that our future marriages remain? How do we establish what the culture calls true love? In his book, *The Meaning of Marriage*, Timothy Keller alludes to three levels of friendship and attraction that are necessary for any relationship to thrive.[13]

- The supernatural friendship
- The natural friendship
- The romantic friendship

The longer I minister to couples, the more I see the vital need to honour these three levels of friendship. Let us see what they are.

THE SUPERNATURAL FRIENDSHIP

As far as relationships are concerned, the supernatural friendship and attraction is a union between two people of the opposite sex based on their mutual spiritual journey. For a relationship to thrive, it is imperative that they have similar spiritual antennae. What does that mean? It means they are both committed to the same God. They are both growing spiritually in the same faith. When this does not happen, the Bible calls it being "unequally yoked" (2 Corinthians 6:14 ESV). We will look at this deeply towards the end of this chapter.

The supernatural friendship in the Christian faith manifests itself in corporate spiritual activity. A supernatural friend is one to whom you can confess your sin. A supernatural friend challenges you to cultivate a deeper obedient walk with God. A supernatural friend is one with whom you can engage in the spiritual disciplines of the faith corporately (prayer, fasting, giving, ministering). The Christian faith is designed in such a way that it needs us to work in relationships. A life partner must be a supernatural friend in order for you to live out your faith effectively. A supernatural friend draws you closer to Christ. The supernatural friendship involves pursuing spiritual mission together. A supernatural friend is concerned about bringing God's Kingdom on Earth as it is in heaven. This is someone who will help further this mission when you get married. Because of this, you must look at your spiritual gifts and all that concerns your purpose on Earth before you settle with someone. You must consider theirs as well. You must ask how coming together will assist bringing about God's Kingdom's purposes here on Earth. Do you and the person interested in you have a supernatural friendship? Many a time, this is the only circle of friendship that some believers look at and believe it will be enough. But there are two more. The natural and the romantic.

THE NATURAL FRIENDSHIP

As far as relationships are concerned, the natural friendship and attraction is a union between two people of the opposite sex based on mutual leisure and preferences. All it takes is to share or engage in similar natural activities.

These activities could range from the books you prefer to read to the hobbies or pastime activities you like. While you may not necessarily have the same natural tastes, a relationship's friendship is built when you enter into your partner's world. You can develop a natural friendship with almost anyone. You can be natural friends with an atheist because of your mutual love for theatre. You could be natural friends with someone from a different religion because of your shared interests in classical music.

It is equally imperative that you develop a natural friendship with the person you plan to marry. From my observation, the fastest way to be someone's friend is to go for the natural. Natural friendships are important for a couple to develop a deep bond that stands in the tough times of a relationship.

THE ROMANTIC FRIENDSHIP

Finally, consider the romantic friendship. Some believers downplay this friendship a lot, yet it is a gift from God. The culmination of this romantic friendship in marriage is in the act of sex. The best way to preserve a romantic friendship is to walk in sexual purity and emotional integrity as you relate with people of the opposite sex. We will deal with this in a later chapter.

The romantic friendship includes the normal physical attraction you may have to your partner. It also involves the five love languages: acts of service, quality time, giving/receiving gifts, physical touch, words of affirmation.[14] It is imperative to know your partner's love language so that you demonstrate affection in a way that builds the relationship. You can at times tell what your love language is by just simply looking at the list. However, we recommend that you read the book or take the test on *www.5lovelanguages.com*.

The romantic friendship can also be cultivated by examining specific gender-based needs such as what Shaunti Feldhahn calls the "fantastic five".[15] This list can help you work on your own relationship, especially if you ask your partner to show you which of the five could do with some improvement. Let us start with the women's fantastic five:

- Take her by the hand.
- Leave her a voice mail message, text message, or email to tell her you love her and are thinking about her.
- Put your arm around her, or your hand on her knee, when you're sitting next to her especially when you're in public.
- Sincerely tell her she's beautiful.
- Pull yourself out of a funk.

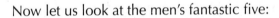

Now let us look at the men's fantastic five:

- Notice his effort and sincerely thank him for it.
- Verbally say "You did a great job at . . . "
- Mention in front of others something he did well.
- Show that you desire him sexually and that he pleases you sexually.
- Make it clear to him that he makes you happy.

Shaunti got her data by interviewing married people. Therefore, some of the things on the list are appropriate only when you are married (like the sexual desire and pleasure for men and the hand on the knee for women). We advocate that such beautiful erotic practices be reserved for their time – in marriage. Outside of that, the relationship will be destroyed by sin. We shall look at that in the chapter on sexual purity. However, this gives you a glimpse of what romance entails for men and women. And even if you are not married you can easily practice the rest and inquire from your partner what would help them feel romantically loved.

TRUE LOVE

While considering the three friendship circles, it is also imperative that you have the right idea of true love. One real test of maturity in a relationship is having the capacity to commit to the relationship after the butterflies have ended. Often, people don't fall out of love; they simply lack the emotional ethic to know that love is a commitment and not just a feeling. The essence of true love, especially in a marriage, is a commitment first and a feeling second – not the other way around.

The world bases love as a feeling first and a commitment second. Just think of Disney! Because of this misplaced order, lots of relationships that begin on feelings end so quickly that the members hardly taste commitment. They jump from relationship to relationship, divorce to divorce, seeking feelings of love. If you ask them why they left the relationship, they say, "We didn't love each other anymore." Yet the truth is, there was no true love in the first place. Why? True love is a commitment first and a feeling second. What existed was a fuzzy emotional thrill that can last no more than two years in an ideal environment. When, after two years, the mushy feelings cease, the person concludes that love has died. This is the relationship between feelings and commitment. Feelings lead to temporal commitment and commitment always leads to lasting feelings.

Biblical love is a commitment to be kept before it is an emotion to be felt. If I obsess over the feeling of love, I may never get to act in love. My affection will be a slave to my emotions. My devotion will be a prisoner to my circumstances. God doesn't need me to feel love towards my spouse so that I can act in love towards her. He expects me to act in love towards her despite my shifting feelings. My commitment to my spouse at the altar trumps my feelings that will alter. The disappointing irony of pursuing euphoria as a motivation to act in love is that the ecstasy burns up and out like a flambé and leaves me empty, waiting for the next circumstantial emotional high. <u>Mature love seeks the good of the other unconditionally.</u>

COMMITMENT ALWAYS LEADS TO LASTING FEELINGS

The rewarding irony of acting in love despite how I feel is that I eventually develop lasting feelings for my partner. I never did like doing dishes growing up. My siblings know this. When I got married though, I realized that I had made a commitment to Turi "for better or for worse". When she once asked me to help her with the dishes, honestly, I was annoyed. I did not feel good about it. But I did the dishes anyway.

That night as I washed and she cooked, we had such an intimate conversation between us. The next time she asked me to do dishes, I did not feel like doing them again. My feelings were ugh! Yet still I did the dishes and we talked again. With time, I realized something – that I enjoyed talking to my wife as I did dishes. I still did not like doing dishes but soon everything changed. I began doing dishes because I enjoyed spending time with her. When she wasn't in the kitchen anymore and asked me to do dishes, I felt like I had lost my incentive to clean the dishes. Who would I talk to now? Still, I committed to do the dishes even when she was not in the kitchen.

Things changed again. I committed to doing the dishes until a time came when I found myself doing dishes even when she wasn't at home! The creepy thing about it is that not only did I not need an incentive to do the dishes, but I also ended up enjoying doing them! I saw that pile of greasy plates smiling at me and I smiled back at them as I dipped them in the hot soapy water.

ROOTS AND FLOWERS

Committing to love someone and overcoming the temporary feelings is not enough though. Your commitment will have more resolve to withstand the waves of feelings if you are committed to something solid. If you commit to a woman's physical beauty, you will lose it when another more attractive woman comes your way. If you commit to a man's bank account, you will lose it when he has a season of financial lack. In your pursuit to marry well, do not let your commitment depend on something temporal. You must make sure to fall in love with someone's roots and not just their flowers; otherwise, you will be thrilled by the blossoming and budding in spring and summer and lose hope in the withering and weathering of fall and winter.

Too many young people make relationship choices based on short-term thrills that fade. Once they get married, they realize they have built a weak foundation for their relationship.

MAKE SURE YOU FALL IN LOVE WITH SOMEONE'S ROOTS AND NOT JUST THEIR FLOWERS.

They imagined the thrill of today would be the pattern of everyday. When the cold season checks in, they realize their priorities in choosing a life partner were upside down. In order to lay a great foundation for a relationship with the opposite sex that leads to marriage, you must ensure that your core values are priority in choosing this person; you must ensure you go for root and not just flowers. One foundational root (among many others) for anyone who is a follower of Jesus Christ is faith. If you are obediently walking with God and you value your faith, start a relationship with someone who does the same.

Be mutually rooted. If you claim to be a believer but are living in disobedience, you will find that your trademark response to God's clear instruction in his Word is always trying to justify what he has clearly spoken against. What you do not realize is that you are trading roots for flowers. When people claim to be born again but they are willing to compromise on their roots in a relationship, it becomes clear that they do not really value their faith. They may tweet their faith, Facebook their faith, and Instagram it with cool Bible verses, but it means nothing if they don't live it out.

Eventually life teaches us that your roots are what keep you going for richer or for poorer, in sickness and in health, until death do you part. The flowers will fade in harsh times, but the roots will keep you growing even in the dreariness of fall and the killer frost of winter. Make sure you fall in love with someone's roots and not just their flowers.

ROOTS VERSUS FLOWERS: CAN I MARRY AN UNBELIEVER?

When we address love, sex, and relationship issues in conferences and events, many professing believers ask us, "Is it okay for me to date or marry an unbeliever?" The answer may seem obvious to many mature followers of Jesus, but for many growing believers, this question ought to be answered well for them to understand why the answer is "No". Often there is a justification to counter the answer that goes like this,

"What if I am dating them to convert them to be a born-again Christian?" Another one goes like this: "My mother is born again but my dad is not born again, and their marriage worked out okay." A third one goes like this: "But I have seen people in church divorce and people in the world stay together." Many of these rejoinders come from believers who are already dating unbelievers or already married to them. In light of this, we recognize the delicate nature of the scenario. However, it doesn't cause us to water down the wisdom of the Scriptures.

The Scriptures are clear concerning this issue. The Bible says in Amos 3:3 "Do two walk together unless they have agreed to do so?" Paul the apostle warned the Corinthian church against intimate relationships with unbelievers.

> Do not be yoked together with unbelievers. For what do righteousness and wickedness have in common? Or what fellowship can light have with darkness? What harmony is there between Christ and Belial? Or what does a believer have in common with an unbeliever? What agreement is there between the temple of God and idols? For we are the temple of the living God. As God has said:
>
>> 'I will live with them
>>> and walk among them,
>> and I will be their God,
>>> and they will be my people' (2 Corinthians
>>> 6:14-16).

Paul also clearly commanded the Corinthians that they were free to marry anyone but only under one condition – that the person they were going to marry was in the Lord (1 Corinthians 7:39). Someone once said to me that their auntie married an unbeliever and their marriage turned out okay. I was quick to caution them as I do you now, that okay is not God's best. Secondly, the exception is not the rule. Many believers hurt from that decision. A marriage that stands in such an instance is by the mercy and grace of God. Thirdly, a Christian marriage has a superior purpose; to reflect the love of Christ and the church. The decision of whom to marry is a fragile one.

But what if the person I want to marry is an unbeliever but is a good person? She doesn't do any of the nasty things that could break a marriage. He is a really good person despite not being born again. Jesus's words to Nicodemus in John 3 can respond to this. Nicodemus is an old, rich, and respected Pharisee of the Jewish high council – the Sanhedrin. Jesus tells him that he cannot see the Kingdom of God (he is not saved from his sins) unless he is born again.

Jesus shocks the readers who go through that passage! You study Nicodemus and realize that he is a typical nice guy. He doesn't drink, he doesn't smoke, and he doesn't sleep around. He is what many would call a good person. He even comes to see Jesus and praises him genuinely unlike those high-nosed Pharisees. Nicodemus doesn't want Jesus dead. In fact, in John 3:2 Nicodemus affirms that Jesus is a true teacher from God. But what does Jesus tell us? Jesus tells us that a man with all the moral, character, and religious qualifications of Nicodemus is not going to heaven.

Jesus unequivocally states that Nicodemus – the moral, upright, respected, and religious leader – MUST be born again!

A CHRISTIAN MARRIAGE HAS A SUPERIOR PURPOSE; TO REFLECT THE LOVE OF CHRIST AND THE CHURCH. But does Jesus know Nicodemus has been studying the Scriptures since he was a kid? Yes, Jesus knows! Does Jesus recognize that

Nicodemus has helped settle disputes between people with his authority? Yes, Jesus knows! Does Jesus realize Nicodemus has been giving to the poor and helping the less fortunate? Yes, Jesus knows! Does Jesus realize that Nicodemus is willing to learn from Jesus unlike the other Pharisees? Yes, Jesus knows! But despite all this, Jesus is telling Nicodemus that it isn't enough to enter heaven with all those medals and golden-boy awards. <u>Good is just not necessarily God.</u>

Nicodemus must be born again. Jesus is basically telling Nicodemus, "All that you have achieved and done up to now amounts to nothing. You need to start from day one afresh." Jesus is telling us that the idea of being born again is *bigger* than moral conformity! It's radically richer than waiting for sex until marriage or not going clubbing and drinking. <u>It's not a call to morality; it's a challenge to submission to God's will (that is greater than human morality).</u> Jesus then explains to Nicodemus that the born-again experience is not a return into one's mother's womb but rather it is a spiritual rebirth! It's the work of the Holy Spirit.

The analogy of new birth affirms a profound truth; that good is not necessarily God. That God's concern is not just for moral uprightness, but for spiritual readiness. If Jesus, the Lamb of God, insists that his bride must be born again, we too must take on that insistence that our partners are not just good, but also full of God.

Well, what if I convert them to Christianity? While this may sound righteous, we must look at it keenly. When a believer wants to convert an unbeliever for the purposes of dating them, their primary concern often is not in the salvation of the unbeliever. <u>Their primary concern is for them to date who they want.</u> <u>The idea of "missionary dating"</u> sanitizes a rather selfish <u>ambition.</u> It's the same front Christians use when gossiping about

other believers in the name of prayer. It has a form of godliness on the surface, but it lacks the power thereof because it is self-seeking; 1 Corinthians 13:5 says love "is not self-seeking."

Also, believers who say they will date an unbeliever to convert him or her shows little respect and worth for the unbeliever. In saying they will convert an unbeliever, they almost quietly state, "I will bring her or him to my level for I consider myself superior to unbelievers." Such a believer makes an unbeliever a "salvation project." The unbeliever is not stupid. The unbeliever can see that the believer is trying to change him or her. The unbeliever is surprised that someone who claims to be heaven bound and filled with the Spirit can miss the basic fact of life that everybody knows: you cannot change people.

Believers who take it upon themselves to convert unbelievers for the purpose of dating them not only think too highly of themselves but also act in selfishness. Their ultimate concern is not for the salvation of the unbeliever but for their own justification of actions. We must judge our motives at all times.

 I have met many believers who went down this path. The unbeliever started conforming just to please them. They went to church. They listened to gospel music. They basically played along. However, it got to a point where the pretence was too much, and they could not keep it up. In some unfortunate instances, they were already married. I tried doing the same thing with a girl I liked and, by the grace of God, it backfired on me. My motivation was selfish and had no concern for the unbeliever.

Growing up I actually believed that I alone ultimately made the choice to be saved. However, the more I studied the Scriptures and listened to sound teachers, I came to see that

this was not true. The Scriptures describe me before salvation as a person who is dead in my sins and transgressions (Ephesians 2:1). Colossians 1:13 says I was in the domain of darkness before Jesus (not me) transferred me into the Kingdom of light. Imagine with me the list of efforts you made to come into this world. Can you name at least five actions of effort? Can you genuinely say that "I am on this planet Earth because I introduced my mother to my father"? Did you cause their meeting? No. Did you cause their night of passionate love? No. Did you cause the fertility of your mother's womb? No. Did you cause your healthy development as a foetus? No.

If we contributed nothing to our physical birth, what makes us think we contributed a sliver to our spiritual birth? Humanity's only contribution to the salvation process is our sins! If you are born again, it is purely out of the mercy and grace that God has for you. You were dead in your sins and transgressions and he made you alive spiritually. If you want to see the dead raised to life, consider this: that your own salvation is a miracle.

One may argue, "I agree that we are saved by grace through faith as stated in Ephesians 2:8-9, but isn't that grace through my faith? Didn't I make the decision to follow Christ?" Well, yes, but you were only able to inevitably and irresistibly "choose" Christ after you were raised from spiritual death. The Word of God was preached to you and you heard it. Jesus said in John 15:16 that we did not choose him but rather, he chose us so that we may bear fruit.

When the Word of God stirred you to respond to Christ, God was choosing you. And since faith comes by hearing the Word of God, you responded to salvation. But do you see that the faith in your salvation was prompted by the Spirit of the Word of God? Without the prompting would you respond? It is as if a patient on their deathbed received resuscitation shocks

and when he comes alive boasts that he is alive because his heart made an effort to respond to the electric shocks. It's absurd. The resuscitation shocks prompted the beating of the heart that led to the revival!

Similarly, the Word of God prompted saving faith that led to salvation. Do you see that if it wasn't for God's generosity of his Word and his Spirit, you would be unable to be revived to faith which wouldn't lead you to salvation? I cannot boast about my salvation as if it is something I achieved because I am saved by the grace of God through faith in Christ (and that faith comes by and from Christ).

What was the point of all that? Are we not talking about dating an unbeliever? Yes, we are. However, none of that is a non sequitur. I said all that to let you know this: "If you cannot bring about your own salvation, what makes you think you will bring about the salvation of a fellow unregenerate?" That is the work and liberty of the Holy Spirit. Last I checked, you and I did not qualify for that job description.

ROOTS VERSUS FLOWERS: FINANCIAL PROWESS AND PHYSICAL ATTRACTION

One of the biggest lies penetrating our culture is that if you want to be a girl worthy of love, you must be worthy of sexual desire. The other side of the coin is that if you want to be a man worthy of love you must have an overflowing bank account. Sexy legs and fancy cars seem to be the way to land a date nowadays. Objectification of people is the one of the biggest hindrances to healthy relationships. Women are reduced to sex objects and men are reduced to success objects. And the outcome in both is that sex and money are used to audition for relationships.

The media sets unrealistic standards for physical beauty for women and financial prosperity for men. Even though women do not voice it, you can see very clearly that women are trying very hard to attain absurd standards of sexual beauty in order to attract and receive love. Similarly, you see men trying to amass wealth to impress women. We will address the men and women separately in future chapters.

Unfortunately, most of the role models of society come from pop culture media and entertainment. And these women promote sexual beauty above character. The men promote financial prosperity before integrity. And as women get induced to believe that tighter jeans will mean a more secure love, the carnal man is watching a piece of meat for him to roast on the fires of lust. And as the men get induced to believe that only money will get them a woman, they postpone marriage until very late in their lives.

OBJECTIFICATION OF PEOPLE IS THE ONE OF THE BIGGEST HINDRANCES TO HEALTHY RELATIONSHIPS.

The Bible would have a word to men; their lives do not consist in having an abundance of things (Luke 12:15). The Bible would also have a word to the women: "Charm is deceptive, and beauty is fleeting; but a woman who fears the Lord is to be praised" (Proverbs 31:30). It adds in 1 Peter 3:3-4:

> Your beauty should not come from outward adornment, such as elaborate hairstyles and the wearing of gold jewellery and fine clothes. Rather, it should be that of your inner self, the unfading beauty of a gentle and quiet spirit, which is of great worth in God's sight.

Is the Bible against money, braided hair, and physical beauty? Of course not. But physical beauty fades and money can't buy love. If physical beauty and financial prosperity could be the cornerstone of great marriages, then Hollywood unions would lead the pack. But they do not. Because inasmuch as physical beauty is compelling and lots of money is exciting, that's just the flowers. The inner beauty that gets brighter is the root. The richness of character is the root. While the beauty of a woman captivates a man, he must be sober enough to realize that it is not meant to last. And a woman must realize that money cannot heal a breaking heart. Flowers can't raise children. Flowers can't remain faithful. Flowers can't grow relationships. Only roots can.

7

MAN ENOUGH

**WHEN I WAS A CHILD, I TALKED LIKE A CHILD,
I THOUGHT LIKE A CHILD, I REASONED LIKE A CHILD.
WHEN I BECAME A MAN, I PUT THE WAYS
OF CHILDHOOD BEHIND ME.
1 CORINTHIANS 13:11**

In this section, I would like to speak to the men. It is not untrue to say that there is a male crisis in the 21st century. Many men do not know what makes them men. Is it our sexual reproductive organs? What identifies you as a man? Identity in a nutshell is the justification for your existence. If you cannot justify it, you will be in a crisis. Many men have their masculinity pegged on temporal circumstances. If you are manly because you can dead lift 200 kgs in the gym, then it's only a matter of time before you grow older and can no longer lift.

If you are manly because you are the best in your field of work, then your masculinity faces extinction when the fresh graduates with newer ideas enter the marketplace. Men in those positions end up sinking into an existential crisis. Masculinity reaches a point of fragility when its foundation is based on something temporary. The answer to true masculinity lies in something permanent.

If you study pop culture you will realize that the world is telling men that they are manly if they have three things. Or, in short, these three things are what the average man lives for: attaining and retaining female attention, financial prosperity, and social dominance. I am going to call these three, girls, gold, and glory. Let me expound. These are the thoughts of a man whose identity rests in any of the three Gs.

Girls: attaining and retaining female attention gives me admiration from other men. Women are sexual accessories to enhance my masculine image. When I am seen with women, I am perceived as manly.

Gold: financial prosperity gives my masculinity freedom, security, power, and love. It grants me the attention of women and it also grants the inevitable envy of fellow men. I feel important because I have money. Without money I'm not manly enough.

Glory: social dominance (fame, respect, titles, status, prestige, possessions, favour, popularity, leadership) gives my masculinity relevance and makes me the alpha male in the room. It is important that I stand out in public for something. If I can't be seen as the guy with the sleekest car, I will be seen as the most humorous one in the room.

This narrative is not new and nobody in the modern 21st century should actually be shocked by this. You may not hear a man verbally articulate those positions on girls, gold, and glory, but you will see it manifested in his behaviour. Let's look at each G.

GIRLS MYTH: FEMALE ATTENTION AND RETENTION MAKES ME A MAN.

Men simply love the ego rush of sitting next to a physically attractive woman. It is a bigger rush if he is at an event and he is identified for being with that woman. He gets a kick out of it by noticing other men notice him with that woman. And often the man desires that the physically attractive woman is beautiful by international standards, across time; this woman is accepted by all cultures as a force of physical beauty.

Now in itself, I believe there is nothing wrong with desiring a beautiful woman. Often, many men peg on a woman's physical attractiveness as an introductory step to get to know her as a person. But there are men who do not care about the second step. They want to remain on the first step – her sexual beauty. Such a man may fear going to the next step because he may not like what he encounters. He wants the youthful face, the nice legs, the slim waist, and the attractive derriere to remain intact. And if they don't, he will leave her and move on to another woman.

In my high school, it was an abomination to go for a school event and not talk to a beautiful girl. If you did, you were celebrated as the man. If you did not, you would be the unfortunate laughing stock of the school. You would then become relegated to being womanly and given the title *breezer*. A breezer was a sissy who did not have the manly courage to walk up to a viciously attractive girl to start a conversation; he instead stood by the sidelines as the cold wind hit him. It was the biggest dread to be called a breezer.

To be deemed manly in my high school, you also needed the skills to keep the girl engaged in conversation and company. If you maintained the company and conversation with a drop-dead-gorgeous female, you were perceived to be so manly that people would talk about it for a week. If you lost her to your schoolmate (we called it slicing) you were not man enough.

But the worst thing (worse than being sliced and worse than being a breezer) was to talk to a plain girl; or one whom testosterone-filled boys would call ugly.

MANY MEN ARE INDOCTRINATED INTO THE CULTURE'S LIE, THAT MANHOOD AND MASCULINITY ARE PEGGED ON HAVING A WOMAN AS A SEXUAL ACCESSORY.

This experience is not new. From a very early point in life, many men are indoctrinated into the culture's lie, that manhood and masculinity are pegged on having a woman as a sexual accessory; a trophy to show off to the world. And this narrative if not addressed, will follow a man into adulthood. As the man grows older, his carnal side is exacerbated when he desires to be identified by more women by his side, and not just one. Even if the sexual attraction of the woman by his side endures, his desire for that ego rush is not satisfied with one. He wants two. And with time, two will be too mainstream. He wants a bevy. One as his neighbour and another as his office mate. One as his jogging partner and another as his desk mate in the class. One as his wife and another as his best friend. He is collecting trophies.

When he is seen to have these women around him while some men have none, he assumes himself a man. When he is perceived to have options (and quality ones at that) while some men are left to settle with the plain females that life's default offers, he feels manly.

On the converse, when the girls don't feel pursued, they expose their sexual body parts to get male attention (but that's a story for the ladies). This idea of manhood is seen in pop culture's music videos: One man in a swimming pool with a bevy of sexually titillating females. He sings of the grandeur of their physical bodies. He speaks of how he wants to make love to that body (not the woman). He speaks of the beauty of the woman's skin colour, but he doesn't do it by showing us her face; he shows us her sexual organs. He speaks of the importance of appreciating women, but he doesn't place plus-sized ones with him or those we would consider plain and unattractive; he instead places those with dramatic sexual appeal and he associates himself with them. In the video the message is clear; these sexual goddesses want him and he has bagged them all.

No wonder many men believe that any woman out there is calling for sexual attention from men to themselves. Where do you think they learned that from? In the movies and music videos. These women are willing to submit sexually to the man's bidding because they desire his big house, his bank account, and his sexual prowess (which he often exaggerates).

We must not be fooled. We know the true intention of those videos. It's not about the woman; it's about her sexual attractiveness. It's not about her personality; it's about her youthful breasts. It's not about her ambition and brains; it's about her willingness to submit to his sexual fantasies and make him look like a man. And this is the bottom line: many men define sexual conquest over women as masculinity. They seek it, pursue it, and even do stupid things to be defined by it. That kind of entertainment only titillates and exacerbates immature masculinity. A man who wants to be free from this false idea of masculinity can start by getting rid of that kind of media and staying clear of it.

I had to delete over 20 gigabytes of movies and television series that sold this false idea of masculinity to me. I was intoxicated by it to the point that I got into a pornography and masturbation addiction. This toxic kind of masculinity is not liberating; it's consuming. The man that wants a great relationship in the future must be willing to pay the price. While everyone is discussing the latest TV series, choose to pay the price. Decide to be outdated in the entertainment scene but relevant as a suitable marriage candidate.

GOLD MYTH: FINANCIAL PROSPERITY MAKES ME A MAN

The second cultural definer of masculinity is financial prosperity. Now I must begin by saying that money meets the following needs in any human being's life:

- Freedom to access a variety of experiences, e.g., buy technology, visit new places, go on holidays
- Security to counter misfortune, e.g., being locked out by the landlord/landlady
- Power to influence people to do our bidding, e.g., service industries
- Love to demonstrate through the giving of gifts, e.g., clearing a hospital bill of a friend

In God's economy, money is a servant to the human being. In the economy of a man whose identity is pegged on money, he is a slave to it. He lives for it because of the things it promises him. He just doesn't want money for freedom to go on a new holiday; he wants freedom to try the most luxurious experiences and to be envied for it. He just does not want money for security over misfortunes; he wants money as a consolation when he cannot avoid misfortunes such as death, disloyalty, and divorce. He does not want money simply to have people serve him where he is incapable; he wants money as a means to control his relationships especially with the opposite sex. He wants to show that since he is the provider, he has the final say. If she leaves, he will buy her back by getting her the new iPhone. If he can afford it, he can afford her.

To him, everyone has a price. He just doesn't want money to demonstrate love to those in need; he wants money to indebt people (especially women) to love him back. And this is the bottom line: many men define financial prosperity as masculinity. It is flaunted by pop culture. If they are impatient when it grows slowly, they will gamble and bet to get it quickly. If they are frustrated when they can't get it legally, they may steal it and pilfer to attain it. Without money, this man feels powerless and less of a man. He feels incapacitated and without any authority. He always attracts the wrong kind of woman. Because he woos her with money, he needs money to keep her. But because the woman's identity is also in having money in order to have a meaningful life, one would almost say that they deserve each other.

GLORY MYTH: SOCIAL DOMINANCE MAKES ME A MAN

I have defined glory as fame, respect, titles, status, prestige, possessions, favour, popularity, and leadership. Let me give examples of glory:

- Wealth, e.g., Bill Gates
- Respect, e.g., Mike Tyson for his legendary boxing career
- Titles, e.g., CEO, Governor, etc.
- Status, e.g., Best rapper 2018, Best something
- Prestige, e.g., studying at Harvard or working for a multinational company

- Possessions, e.g., having a car or your own house
- Favour and popularity, e.g., adored and liked by many people
- Fame, e.g., known and revered by many people
- Leadership, e.g., affecting and influencing other people's behaviour

These things are not devils. They are good tools to help useful causes. However, they can be abused when a man derives his identity from them. He is most likely to be intoxicated with an abnormal degree of self-importance. And if he meets another man who threatens this throne, he will try to embarrass him with his glory in order to remain the only alpha in the room. He will buy the other man's girlfriend a drink that the boyfriend can't afford. He will ostentatiously place his car keys on the table for everyone to see that he owns the Mercedes parked outside.

He will consider himself better than others. He will imagine himself to be the most important and relevant man in the room and he will feel threatened when other men take the limelight and he is not recognized. He will be upset when his glory is not recognized. He must have the final say in a matter. He will correct people when introduced as "Ernest" and not "Dr Ernest." I once heard of an elderly bishop who gave a youthful clergy a tongue-lashing because the young man referred to the old man as "Pastor" and not "Bishop."

About two years ago, I was with a friend who introduced me to a local Kenyan celebrity whom I did not recognize. The man gave me a dirty look and sulked throughout the meeting, ignoring me completely and dismissing my contributions to the project we were working on. A man with his identity as his glory may even fool himself to think his opinion is God's truth;

look at the number of celebrities who talk authoritatively on matters they know nothing about.

Look at the way politicians speak authoritatively on scientific matters, yet most know nothing on the subject. Look at how authoritatively Hollywood stars comment on marriage and parenting like seasoned experts. It's the delusion of glory. And this is the bottom line: many men define glory as masculinity. They seek it, pursue it, and militantly oppose anyone who prevents them from accessing it.

IT'S ALL ABOUT POWER

Girls, gold, and glory can be summarized in one word for the man who derives his identity from them: POWER. These things grant him power. Most men when seeking to attract, maintain, and retain a woman in a romantic relationship depend on power. They know the narrative of the culture: The more power you have, the more masculine you are perceived to be by both men and women. But there are two major downsides to having girls, gold, and glory define your masculinity.

THE DOWNSIDE OF THE THREE GS

When a man has his identity in the three Gs, he sets himself up for failure in life. He is intimidated by fellow men who are faring better than he is in any of those three Gs. He cannot stand up against evil people in society with the three Gs; he feels incompetent and unmanly to do so. The man who has his identity in the three Gs is on a losing streak even if he gets what he wants.

Girls: The girls he uses as sexual trophies will eventually lose their sexual beauty. And if he lives for this, he may end up making foolish decisions that involve him getting disease and having a horrible marriage as he pursues the latest big bust in town.

Gold: In multiple ways, his money can disappear or lose value. His money cannot last forever. And even if it should, his money will not carry him past death. The more money he makes, the more money he leaves behind when he dies (Which could even be his 30's – death respects nobody).

Glory: Glory fades. Today you are the top artist; tomorrow nobody fills your concerts. Today you have the corner office job; tomorrow you are sick and they let you go. Today you have the latest iPhone; tomorrow Apple releases another. Today you have a title; tomorrow you are demoted or you retire.

However, the worst effect is in the area of relationships, when this man meets an empowered woman.

1. The Sexually Pure Woman

The man with his identity tied to having a woman by his side meets an attractive woman who pursues sexual purity and who respects her body. He becomes frustrated because he cannot use her as a sexual accessory. This woman has learned that the worth of her womanhood does not come from her sexual appeal but from her character. She becomes a difficult woman to conquer as a sexual trophy. He praises her physical form, and he gets nothing but disgust and disrespect from her. She dresses modestly; she is a wonder to him because he has not been exposed to her nudity. She can see through his act; he sees her as a piece of meat to advertise and enhance his masculinity. She will not bow to it. She is a difficult woman because she pursues purity. His last resort:

- Insult her: He will try to intimidate her just as he is intimidated by her.
- Abuse her: He will forcefully violate her sexual boundaries to demean her.

- Bad-mouth her: He will spread false rumours about her to assassinate her character and virtue (which he cannot keep up with).

2. The Financially Independent Woman

The man with his identity in his money meets a woman who makes more money that he does, and he is intimidated. He cannot buy her when they have a fallout. She has access to more freedom and security through her own money; he therefore cannot console himself with his wealth when he faces a divorce or when the woman walks out. He feels he cannot have the final say in a matter because he is no longer the provider. He cannot indebt her to love him. In fact, he feels emasculated for all the times that he owes her. His last resort:

- Replace her: He will seek a younger woman with little or no money whom he can impress and feel manly enough. This may result in him cheating to satisfy his ego.
- Abuse her: Because his money is dumb, he may let his fists do the talking. He will physically hit her to force his way and make her subservient to his inflated ego.
- Leave her: If he cannot hit her, he will leave her and say something akin to, "She is not my type."

3. The Alpha Female

The man with his identity in his fame, respect, titles, status, prestige, possessions, favour, popularity, and leadership will be dismayed when he meets a woman with greater fame, richer respect, bigger titles, larger status, grander prestige, more possessions, infinite favour, more popularity, and better leadership. He cannot impress her with his job title. He cannot lure her with his big name and fame. He cannot excite her with his achievements. His last resort:

- Compete with her: He will try to outdo her glory to prove his manliness.
- Embarrass her: Just as he does with men who threaten his glory, he will do the same to her to try make her subservient.

POWER-BASED MASCULINITY VERSUS VALUE-BASED MASCULINITY

If your masculinity is pegged on power, it will never stand. Your masculinity must be pegged on something bigger. The only thing bigger than a man is a cause he is willing to die for. And at the heart of that cause are values. Freedom is a value. Peace is a value. Our values can outlive us. Here is the contrast between power and values.

Sexual Conquest (Girls) Versus Values

Values triumph sexual conquest any day. A man who has his identity in values respects a woman's sexuality. He is not intimidated by a woman with sexual purity. He encourages her femininity and protects her purity. A man with values chooses a woman for what's between her ears not what's between her arms. It's not that sexual attraction is not important to this man; it is. It's only that he has the wisdom to know that beauty does not raise kids and build a marriage. He has the wisdom to know that he needs a woman to grow old with and not a trophy to display. This kind of woman will feel secure and loved and remain with this man because his values are out to shield her not tear her down and abuse her.

Financial Prosperity (Gold) Versus Values

Values triumph financial prosperity any day. It's easy to make an extra lump sum of money. It's not easy to control your temper. It's easy to buy her a car on Valentine's Day; it's not easy to remain faithful. A man with truckloads of money may impress a materialistic girl but only a man with solid values will impress a real woman. The man with gold as his identity will imagine that buying her a gift on her birthday will compensate for flirting with a girl. A man with values as his identity knows well that remaining faithful is the least he could do to demonstrate his masculinity. A man with values as his identity will never buy his woman to follow him; he will inspire her to follow him.

A woman married to such a man will willingly submit to him because his values protect her, even from himself. She has an assurance that this man will protect her femininity even if it means denying himself. She will give honour to the man even if he earns less than she does. She may earn more, but she will willingly allow this man to be called the head of the family because he inspires leadership and he does not think it can be bought.

A man with values as his identity will use financial prosperity to build his woman, not to crush her. A man with value-based identity may start off by earning more than his woman, but he will not lose his leadership mantle the day he loses his job and has to depend on her income.

Often in such cases, a man with values as his identity will steadily rise to prosperity because he does not see a financially successful woman as a threat but as a partner. He does not see her as a danger but as an advantage to his future family. Instead of leaving her, he will stay by her side and become great as well.

Social Dominance (Glory) Versus Values

A man with glory as his identity may be respected by a woman (but only as long as he has the glory), but a man with values as his identity will be respected by the woman unconditionally. It is one thing to be respected. It is another thing to be worthy of respect. Men with their identity in their glory use their power to make people respect them. They announce it; they correct those who have their titles wrong; they use passive aggression to get recognized. A man whose identity is in his values is worthy of respect. He loves his wife to submission; he does not command her to submit. And he never panics that he will cease being respected because values never fade. Values never run out. They are timeless and consistent.

Values are the stuff that keep a marriage till death do them part. Values prevent a man from hitting a woman, cheating on her, embarrassing her, competing with her, replacing her, leaving her, insulting her, and bad-mouthing her. A man with values as his identity will celebrate the glory of his woman and not be threatened by it.

A FEW FACTS ABOUT VALUE-BASED MASCULINITY

Before I define it and share its origin, here are a few facts about value-based masculinity.

Value-based masculinity, as opposed to power-based masculinity (three Gs) is what this world needs. It's what many marriages need. It's what many leadership positions need. It's what our politics needs. It's what our schools need. Without it, humanity is a world of beasts and brutes.

Value-based masculinity does not dismiss sexual attraction (girls), financial prosperity (gold), and social dominance (glory) entirely. Men with value-based masculinity value sexual attraction, financial prosperity, and social dominance but they don't make gods out of them. Value-based masculinity knows that manliness is not about chasing girls but about leading men. Value-based masculinity knows that manliness is not about making money but about making a difference. Value-based masculinity knows that manliness is not about social dominance but humble service. Values don't dismiss the beauty of sexuality; they honour it instead of pillaging it. Values don't dismiss the importance of money; they refine it. Values don't dismiss the usefulness of social dominance; they manage it.

Value-based masculinity gives a man confidence. Power-based security (three Gs) gives a man cockiness. A man with value-based masculinity is secure about himself because he is self-aware. He is secure about his intentions with women. He is secure about his finances without being intimidated by that of others. He is secure about his purpose and vision.

VALUE-BASED MASCULINITY, AS OPPOSED TO POWER-BASED MASCULINITY (THREE GS) IS WHAT THIS WORLD NEEDS.

The Origin of Value-based Masculinity

But how do we get these values? Do we just decide that we will be good men, patient men, generous men, etc.? No. In fact, self-imposing these characteristics to try and attain value-based masculinity is the worst thing you can do as a man. You will burn out. Why? Because value-based masculinity is incompatible with our sinful human heart. The Bible tells us that our hearts are deceitful and beyond cure (Jeremiah 17:9). A heart like that (which is in every man and woman) cannot adopt value-based masculinity. It has no desire to do so.

A heart like that is bent on selfishness and sinfulness. In order to attain value-based masculinity, you must understand that values have a value-giver. And we must ask that value-giver to give us a heart compatible with his superior form of masculinity. Introducing the fourth G.

GOD THE VALUE GIVER

Every source of value that does not stem from God is a thief or a poor imitator. A majority of our countries' constitutional values stem from the Ten Commandments. The moral stand of activists stems from our God-given conscience (Romans 2:14-15). Only a higher being with a higher power allows anyone to have the moral right to say that some things are wrong and some are right. If this moral right to say so comes from one's convenience and benefit, then right and wrong become relative issues.

But the man with value-based masculinity knows that absolutes are genuine. That rape is wrong. That murder is wrong. That stealing is wrong. And he does not just uphold the ones that are easy to agree with. He comes down all the way to the ones that the world disagrees with. He stands by these unpopular ones too: that homosexuality is wrong, that any kind of sexual activity outside the marriage institution is wrong, that sensual thoughts are wrong. He has no grey areas.

Any kind of masculinity that is not based on the big G, God, is at best thievery and will never last because it will frequently intermarry with worldly and secular, power-based masculinity. It will be faithful as long as it is not tempted. It will be confident as long as it is not disrespected. It will be a good father as long as people are watching. Genuine value-based masculinity is what it is because God empowers it; he wills it in a man that surrenders to him and receives his Holy Spirit. And for a man to have the Spirit, he must start by admitting that he is not manly. He then must see that his lack of manliness, his sinfulness, and deceitful heart cannot help itself. He needs a Saviour. And for that man, Christ Jesus died and took away his sin. For that man, Christ allows his Holy Spirit to reside in him. For that man, Christ guides him every day. For that man, Christ promises to glorify him after he dies so that his masculinity goes beyond the grave.

The path to value-based masculinity is to look at the bigger man, Jesus Christ. The man who created all the girls in the world and yet honours each of them. The man who owns the universe and yet chooses a life of a local peasant to save your soul. "For you know the grace of our Lord Jesus Christ, that though he was rich, yet for your sake he became poor, so that you through his poverty might become rich" (2 Corinthians 8:9). The man with all the glory in all of history yet he gives it up on the cross just to justify you and glorify you. Submit to this man. Submit to the big G and the three Gs will make sense.

I will wrap up with a personal story. I had my masculinity wrapped around gold for a while. Until I saw that value-based masculinity was the real manhood. When my wife Waturi first met me, I was 18 going on 19. I was dependent on my parents' pocket money. I couldn't match my shoes and my shirt to save my life. I was free-spirited and outgoing – she was melancholic and reserved. But one thing we had in common is that we admitted to being sinners, saved and changed by the grace of Christ. I knew I wanted to marry her. There was another man interested in her. He was a pilot and drove to school. He made overt moves to win Turi over, but she never budged. I was miles away from owning any vehicle and earning a six-figure salary like the pilot.

The closest I got to financial prosperity was a job I applied for as a French teacher while in campus.[16] They paid me 12,000 KES (about 120 USD) a month to teach basic French. This amount of cash was a gold mine for a student who was still receiving pocket money. But it was pocket change compared to the pilot's salary. However, Turi still chose me. Many ladies in her position would run for the money.

I once asked Turi what she saw in me. She said I may not have had all the money in the world, but she saw a hard worker, a man who feared God, and potential instead of presents. It takes a woman of God to see that. There is a phrase my wife always says to me. It is this: I will always choose you. She affirms the decision she made back then in campus. She had no idea I would be where I am today. So we say to the ladies: marry a man with a vision, not a man with a television. And I can testify that resources always follow vision. That cancels the fear of poverty for any woman. When your marriage is breaking in the middle of the night, a Mercedes S class cannot fix it, but a man of vision submitted to Christ can.

8

GIRL POWER

**CHARM IS DECEPTIVE, AND BEAUTY IS FLEETING; BUT A WOMAN WHO FEARS THE LORD IS TO BE PRAISED.
PROVERBS 31:30**

In this section, we will speak to the women. We described the male identity crisis using the three Gs. We will describe the female identity crisis using what we call the three Bs. Just like the men we talked about, many women have pegged their femininity on a fleeting identity – something that will not hold them for too long. In our time in the ministry, we have seen many women succumb to pop culture's definition of femininity. They are the three Bs – boys, beauty, and brains. In short, many women only feel secure enough in their womanhood when they possess these things over and above others. The mindset behind the three Bs can be summarized like this.

- Boys: Attaining and retaining male attention means I am womanly. The more men that desire me, the more womanly I am. The more dates I get from men, the more admirable I will be to other women.

- Beauty: I am queen when I am the most physically attractive. It also grants me the attention of men and makes me the envy of fellow women.

- Brains: I can do it all by myself. I do not need the help of others to be successful, especially a man. I will be the first woman. I will show them that I am smarter than they are.

These three Bs are embedded deeply in the femininity of the average woman in our culture, but they are poor foundations for female identity. Let us look at each of them keenly.

BOYS: MALE ATTENTION AND RETENTION MAKES ME WOMANLY

Pop culture has told women that the attention of men qualifies them to be womanly. It is seen in our famous stories – Cinderella gets Prince Charming. In the celebrity music videos, the centre stage is a woman and men who desire her flock to her. They do her bidding. In the soap operas, Maria is pursued by many men. Or in the chick-flick films, the quiet introvert girl who puts on bulky spectacles, large t-shirts, and baggy jeans eventually gets noticed for her real attractiveness by the hunk in the football team. This narrative of pop culture tells women that male attention is the endgame.

You will often find two kinds of girls in an average urban setup. There is the first girl who is always asked on dates by men. She will have three coffee dates in one week with three different men. She may even have turned down two because she could not handle all of it. She loves this attention because it feeds her identity of being liked by men. A certain girl we knew had trouble accepting the proposal of one fine man to be his girlfriend. They were both believers and they shared the same values and they both seemed to be very much in love with one another. She turned him down. When we asked her why, she said that she did not want to lock herself out of the market too soon. We later found out that she was going on dates with other men. She feared that saying yes to this one would mean no more dates with the others. She loved the thrill of the chase, but she never wanted to settle. She knew that being someone's girlfriend would mean no more attention from the other men. Despite her desire to be wife material, she cannot deal with the commitment to one man because that would mean the loss of attention of several men.

POP CULTURE TELLS WOMEN THAT MALE ATTENTION IS THE ENDGAME.

The second kind of girl gets hardly asked out on dates. She may envy the girl who has several dates and even try to get help from her. When she does get a chance to be with a man in a relationship, she may end up clinging too closely to him. She may be smothering and overly protective because she desires his attention badly. Her identity is in being liked by men and she cannot imagine losing the one that she has. This second girl with this pop-cultural identity may end up being overly possessive of her man.

The first girl would look at the second girl and disdain her for being too easily available and clingy. The second girl may look at the first girl and disdain her for not being appreciative of a man. However, both girls are similar. They share the same idols – boys. The first girl does not want commitment because it will deny her male attention. The second girl wants commitment because without it she won't get any male attention. They both deeply crave male attention. Their expressions may differ, but their heart is the same.

Now, the attention of men is not sinful. It is a good thing in and of itself. It makes a woman feel special and attractive.

But when the attention of men becomes an ultimate thing then you have trouble. When it becomes an ultimate thing, you will end up with women who are bent to have their men on a leash.

The first kind of woman will be upset when the men stop asking her out on dates. I know of one woman who met men in their houses and made out with them but never had sexual intercourse. She would in fact state that sex outside marriage is a sin and tell these men that she could not go further. In truth, she was keeping these men on a leash. She wanted them to keep coming back but to never get it. This way she would maintain their attention and retention. She knew very well that if she were to give in to sex, the average male would be done with her.

The second kind of woman who gets into a relationship with a man will compromise her values to keep the man. In Kenya, it has been reportedly common for such a girl to go to the man's house to clean it, cook for him, sleep over, and even give him sex the whole weekend so that she can maintain him. If the relationship fails, she may get desperate and depressed.

When male attention is sober, a woman can enjoy it moderately. When it is ultimate, it will be the death of her. Both these women will struggle with rejection from men. For the first woman, rejection will make her feel immensely unattractive. For the second one, rejection will make her feel desperately lonely.

BEAUTY: PHYSICAL ATTRACTIVENESS MAKES ME A WOMAN

Our culture is constantly bombarding women with images of the perfect women. Movies from Hollywood show slim women with gorgeous faces as the damsels that men die for. The beauty products industry is hinged on this narrative and perpetuates it. The next fitness program, the next cream that will make your skin lighter, the next diet plan, etc. are all telling women one thing – you need to maintain youthfulness and beauty in order to be accepted. Certain modern problems reflect this truth. Anorexic women are killing their health in the pursuit of the perfect body. Those with the money are committed to using plastic surgery to maintain a youthful look. There have been several cases of plastic surgeries that have destroyed the health of women, but all these are ignored in the pursuit of the fountain of youth.

It is often joked that you should never ask a woman her age. This pop-culture humour veils the silent truth – many women define their identity with their beauty. If I get older, I get wrinkles. If I get wrinkles, I get enrolled with the grandmas. And no man wants to marry a grandma. This debilitating identity struggle causes many women to panic as they think of marriage. They strongly believe that a more youthful look means higher chances of marriage. The problem is that it feeds directly into the male identity crisis of *girls*. These two identities catch men and women in a horrible symbiotic dance that often ends in early divorce cases.

When we were dating, one of our friends who was a believer was dating a non-believer. Surmise it to say she was a very pretty girl who had received many advances from men. Her boyfriend was also a hunk. In fact, he had been the Adonis that caused many women to melt in his presence. These two were a perfect match. But we knew the man did not share the values that our friend had. They were sexually active outside of marriage and she was convicted that she was sinning in accordance with her Christian faith. The relationship looked great on the outside, but in reality, they were fighting and

POSTING A BIBLE VERSE NEXT TO A SEXUALLY TITILLATING PHOTO DOES NOT CLEAN UP THE MOTIVE.

having a hard time. When she asked us for advice, we told her to end the relationship on account of Christ. She said she knew it was the right thing to do but she had a reservation. We asked her what the reservation was. This was her response, "But our babies will be so cute." We laughed at what we thought was light-hearted humour only to be sobered afterwards by her serious face. She was actually serious. What makes a woman willing to stay in a difficult dating relationship simply because there is a prospect of preserving her gene pool? The answer is *boys* – an identity that makes her believe that without it she is nothing.

You see this identity in girls on social media. There is a thirst to get likes, comments, and reactions by posting pictures that show their physical beauty. A little cleavage here, a bit of the thigh there, a booty short, a smiling face in perfect sunlight, etc. What is often the motive of these posts? To be seen, recognized, admired, loved, appreciated, and accepted because of one's physical attractiveness. One of the things that we often see with Christian women is their attempt to dilute the truth about this identity by posting a Bible verse next to a sexually titillating photo of themselves. But the Bible verse does not clean up the motive.

Physical beauty is not a bad thing; it is not sinful. It is a good thing because it is God's creation. In fact, God used the physical attraction of Queen Esther to fulfil his purposes for Israel. It was the physical beauty of Abigail that endeared David to her wisdom. But when physical attraction is idolized, it ushers in evil. In Genesis, the fallen angels had intercourse with women because they were enthralled by their physical attractiveness. The result of that union was a race of metahumans called the Nephilim. These Nephilim became a thorn in humanity and God had to destroy them in the flood. The remaining strains of their DNA were found in the giants in the land of Canaan. All this trouble because of a pretty face and a good body.

BRAINS: INDEPENDENCE MAKES ME A WOMAN

The feminist movement is largely pegged on this identity. Beyoncé sang that girls run the world. The famous slogan states that what a man can do a woman can do better. The other states that behind every successful man is a woman. What is the narrative here? It is simple; that women have brains and that they can contribute. This identity is often not bent towards making the world a better place. It is often bent towards selfish competition and proving to be better than all others, especially men. The expression of brains for women often looks like this:

- Brainy enough to make my own money so I don't need a man
- Brainy enough to be respected in my career field by beating many men
- Brainy enough to earn a commonly assumed male title, e.g., CEO, Dr
- Brainy enough to make history, e.g., first woman to . . .
- Brainy enough to have my own possessions, e.g., having a car or your own house
- Brainy enough to lead a team of men

Those accolades are good in and of themselves. However, with this narrative, those accolades only matter by comparing themselves to others. Women with this identity are not satisfied with being successful women, period. They want to be women who are more successful than men or than other women. The narrative needs competition in order to have its identity fuelled. Women with this identity are often out to prove that they are not just pretty but they also have brains. Parts of the human body do not call attention to themselves unless there is something wrong with them. You never hear someone say, "My elbows feel great today! Wow! I have the best elbows!" You do not notice your elbows unless there is something wrong with your elbows. Either they are scraped, injured, exposed through a hole in your clothes, or affected in one way or another. To randomly call for attention to a part of your body is to admit that this part of the body is either distended or hurt. And so it is with many women with this identity. Their prowess has either been hurt, demeaned, or challenged, and they feel that they have to compensate for it by competing and proving their worth.

This narrative causes women to not only compete, but also to disdain fellow women who have embraced what would seem to be non-competitive options. Women who choose to have several children, or choose to become housewives, or work as soccer moms are seen as unambitious, lazy, and weak. Yet those options do not define those women in any such way. The woman with an identity in her brains can often be insufferable in relationships. The kindness of men is received as insults. Conversations often centre around her accolades and achievements. However, these women often have cognitive dissonance when natural desires such as getting married, having children, and rearing a family conflict with their ambitions. They may also struggle with biblical imperatives for women such as submission to husbands and playing the role of helper. They do not measure their strength based on what they offer but rather, based on what they offer over others. This unfortunate view makes them often miss out on the true potential of what they have. They use their best energy to compete instead of to achieve.

Like boys and beauty, brains are not a bad thing. We need smart women. Women are not second-class citizens in God's Kingdom. They are not unimportant. We see God use smart women like Deborah to offer spiritual leadership to Israel. Smart women like Esther were used to offer political leadership to Israel. Smart women like the Queen of Sheba were used as important ambassadors to their nation. But when brains become the ultimate thing, women get into cliques that look down on fellow women. They become unteachable in the presence of men who could truly help them. Their ambitious desire to compete prevents them from addressing the wounds in their lives, especially those caused by men.

IT'S ALSO ALL ABOUT POWER

Like the three Gs, the three Bs are all about women having power. The attention and retention of boys is power. Beauty gives women social clout – power. Brains are a demonstration of power over others. And as you have seen, this kind of identity fails to stand. Like men, women need a values-based identity. Where does that come from?

BRIDE OF CHRIST

The three Bs cannot give women identity. Women can only draw lasting identity from understanding that they are the Bride of Christ. Like the men, women get their identity from their Creator first in order for them to enjoy boys, beauty, and brains.

Boys Versus Bride of Christ

A woman must see that God is so enthralled by her and devoted to her that he sent his Son to draw her into his Kingdom. God takes away the sin of the woman and calls her his bride. Every woman must see that without Christ, she is sinful and wretched. There is nothing attractive about sin. But God in his mercy sent his Son to take up all her sin and to die on her behalf. Remember, Jesus died for you. Your boyfriend can only faint for you. There is no man like Christ. And once you have him in your heart, the rejection of men will not be a sting. At the same time, you will not die because of their lack of attention on you. You have the attention of the King already!

Before I got married, I (Turi) had this deceptive expectation: *When I get married, I will feel whole, complete, and satisfied.* I know this seems really gullible, but I did not realize that I was unconsciously expecting my husband to make me feel complete. I had fantasies of how he would melt at the sight of me, how he would slay all the monsters that would emotionally harm me, and how he would bring to a pleasant end my struggle with sexual abstinence!

Granted, my husband is my biggest supporter, listener, and cheerleader. I thank him for questioning my doubts, cheering me on, and encouraging me to develop my gifts and abilities. However, my expectations made an idol out of Ernest. My sense of worth was hinged on his acceptance of me. No human being can play that role in your life. Trust me, I know; I'm an HR recruiter! Only the God of the gospel, Jesus, can. In Christ, we get our sense of worth. How? Christ Jesus accepts us while we are sinners and does not reject us when he sees our worst. Many women give their boyfriends and fiancés the status of saviour. This ends up burdening the relationship unnecessarily.

YOU HAVE THE ATTENTION OF THE KING ALREADY!

You begin to demand from your man what only Christ can give you. <u>As a result, you crush him with your expectations and he crushes you with his imperfections.</u> You cannot enjoy a relationship where your identity comes from your partner.

Having your identity as the bride of Christ will also help you not compromise in your selection of a man to marry. I always wanted to get married, raise a family, and live happily ever after. I prepared for this from an early age. I learned skills that prepared me to be a good homemaker. I even took Home Science as a subject in high school to improve my cooking and sewing skills. I wanted my husband to look forward to coming home to a well-cooked hot meal. If he was a bag of bones, his weight gain would be attributed to my cooking expertise! Win! In essence, my deepest desire was the approval and delight of my husband (boys).

As I was weaving myself into the fabric of being wife-material, I was also setting up an image for the man I wanted: focused, hardworking, smart, financially steady, emotionally available for me and the kids, a celebrant of weddings and birthdays, a man who made me laugh, a man strongly attracted to me, and finally, a gentleman (kind to women – treats his mother, sisters, or female colleagues with love and kindness). That was the man – a good man! I was convinced that once I met a good man, the rest of my life would fall into place.

However, I realized that I had set my hope on a utopian life. That kind of life does not exist – at least not yet. It soon became clear that life will be drizzled with suffering and problems; money does run out, sickness does occur, misfortunes befall everyone, and my purpose in life cannot be centred on idolising marriage. I realized that my expectations were far off from reality. A man who would keep the vows of marriage (for better or for worse, in sickness and in health, in riches and in poverty) needed to be more than just a good man; he needed to be a godly man – one dependent humbly on the grace of God. Good was not enough. Good was not God.

There are many good men that you will meet but they are not necessarily godly men. I have talked to many women who feel that a man's moral compass can compensate for his lack of godliness. Some even tell me that they have seen better-behaved men in the world than in the church. Dear sister, let me help you navigate some of these thoughts. A good man is limited by his own moral record to love a woman, but a godly man is challenged by the love of Christ. A good man's moral compass is nothing compared to the unconditional love of Christ. The love of men will wane, but the love of Christ will stand. When we advocate for godly men over simply good men, we are asking you to trust Christ in the believing man. You must also realize that not all saved brothers are meant for you to marry. Some are undergoing sanctification and still have some maturing to do. A mature godly man will love beyond himself. This is because Christ lives inside of him through the Holy Spirit. Jesus stopped at nothing to love us – he literally died for us! A godly man would be stirred in his spirit to emulate that.

A godly man is also a man under perfect authority. Ladies, you do not want to marry a man who is not under perfect authority. Some of the biggest issues you will face in life need the supernatural wisdom of Christ. A merely good man cannot give you that. A sincerely godly man is God's provision for that, especially since men are called to be the leaders of the home. Thankfully, when I met my husband, he was a godly man – a trait that made our journey to the altar rich and beautiful! That's my prayer for you – that you move beyond the deception of a good man who ticks the list by society's standards and instead strive for a godly man. If you meet a godly man who may not have all his things together, but he is making strides towards settling down and progressing and has focus, that's a man to keep! The grit that is needed for a husband in marriage is not goodness but godliness.

Beauty Versus Bride of Christ

A woman must see that she is beautiful beyond her physical body. 1 Peter 3:3-5a states:

> Your beauty should not come from outward adornment, such as elaborate hairstyles and the wearing of gold jewellery or fine clothes. Rather, it should be that of your inner self, the unfading beauty of a gentle and quiet spirit, which is of great worth in God's sight. For this is the way the holy women of the past who put their hope in God used to adorn themselves.

The beauty of the bride of Christ gets more fair and youthful with time. It is the beauty of the Spirit. The Bible says we were dead in our sins and transgressions before we were born again. But after we were born again, we were raised to new life. Christ turned us from corpses to brides. He is our beautifier! And the manifest quality of that beauty is our character, ladies. We may put on lipstick, but if we use our lips to spread gossip, we lose our beauty. We may pierce our tongues, but if we insult and clap down at people, we have lost our beauty. We may polish our nails, but if we do not polish our patience and kindness, we remain ugly. We may apply foundation on our faces, but if we do not have the foundation of Jesus, we are cracked and ugly. Our inner selves should have the unfading beauty of character in Christ and this is of great worth in God's sight.

Also, you cannot depend on your man to know you are beautiful and useful. That should only come from your Creator. Through God's word, I was affirmed that I was pretty, witty, and bright because God said so. Psalm 139:13-14 says, "For you created my inmost being; you knit me together in my mother's womb. I praise you because I am fearfully and wonderfully made; your works are wonderful, I know that full well." It is important that God's Word affirms your beauty and worth in his eyes. You will only be the strong woman you need to be by seeking worth in God's eyes and not your husband's. When you feel beautiful on the inside, you will radiate on the outside. I trusted God and surrendered to him each day. God is the ultimate husband that makes you more beautiful. When I turned to him for my worth, he sanctified my character to be as that of Christ. As God sanctified me, my mind was renewed. My identity came from his love for me. This new identity purified my longing for the gift of sex. Before

YOU DON'T CRAVE FAST FOOD WHEN YOU ARE SATISFIED WITH A GOURMET MEAL.

that, my reason for chastity was based on fear – fear of getting pregnant, fear of getting a disease, and even fear of my own strict dad! As God worked on my character, I realized that these reasons were flimsy and without conviction. My desires changed; I developed a new conviction to live sexually pure out of love for the God of the gospel who laid down his life for me. I wanted to honour God with my body which is the temple of the Holy Spirit. Is your identity defined by a mortal's acceptance of you? Men will change, but Jesus Christ remains the same yesterday, today, and forever (Hebrews 13:8). The gospel of Jesus liberates you not only from the desperation to be esteemed by people, but also from the need of it. You don't crave fast food when you are satisfied with a gourmet meal.

Brains Versus Bride of Christ

If you have your identity in your work, ladies, your sinful human heart will always compel you to do two things: to look down at people without that degree or standard of work and to revere those with greater degrees and standards of work. If you have your identity in anything finite, your sinful human heart will always compel you to do two things: to look down at those without that finite thing and to revere those with it. The gospel of Jesus compels you to lock your identity on something infinite that has nothing to do with you – the finished work of the cross. You cannot look down on anyone without it because Christ offers his salvation to anyone that comes to him (even those that you think don't deserve it). You cannot look down on anyone who hasn't received it because you know that Christ's salvation is not meritorious but out of sheer grace; you got it by nothing you did. You cannot revere those with it because you understand that they only received it by virtue of being sinners. An identity in the gospel does not bow down to the compulsions of the sinful heart; it cures the sinful heart. The bride of Christ can enjoy the brains that God gives her without selfish competition. And we see that clearly in the Proverbs 31 woman.

> Her husband has full confidence in her
> and lacks nothing of value.
> She brings him good, not harm,
> all the days of her life.
> She selects wool and flax
> and works with eager hands.

She is like the merchant ships,
>   bringing her food from afar.

She gets up while it is still night;
>   she provides food for her family
>   and portions for her female servants.

She considers a field and buys it;
>   out of her earnings she plants a vineyard.

She sets about her work vigorously;
>   her arms are strong for her tasks.

She sees that her trading is profitable,
>   and her lamp does not go out at night.

In her hand she holds the distaff
>   and grasps the spindle with her fingers
>   (Proverbs 31:11-19).

One way to track your idols as a woman is to look at the emotions that spiral out of control. In those action movies, the police are often told to pursue a fleeing suspect but never to open fire to kill. Why? The information that the suspect has is valuable. The suspect is better off alive than dead. It's the same with your uncontrollable emotions, dear believer. When they go off uncontrollably, they betray their connection to a spiritual crime. Pursue them; do not ignore them. Your uncontrollable emotions are often working for some idols. What are idols? Idols are God-substitutes. They are finite things that promise your soul lasting significance, security, and acceptance. The crime lab of your quiet time will show evidence that only God can give that. These idols are drug lords and kingpins in your life. Don't let the uncontrollable emotions get away. Pursue them, find them, arrest them, and bring them back to the station for interrogation. Do not kill the uncontrollable emotions; they are better off alive than dead. When you get the information you need, take the uncontrollable emotions to a correctional facility. Afterwards, execute an attack and bring down the kingpin idols. There is only one mayor in the town of your life, and that's the Lord Jesus!

HAPPILY EVER AFTER? NO, STRONGER EVER AFTER

To sum this all up, I would like to share a letter I wrote to my younger deceived self.

Dear Turi,

I see you in Chemistry class, 17 years old and daydreaming about your marriage. Anyway, you have *the list*! Who doesn't? He must be a mix of Alejandro from the soap *Cuando Seas Mia* and a bit of Justin Timberlake. Who does not want mixed-race children with beautiful hair?

Fast forward several years and you are very happily married to a cute, charming, God-fearing, sensitive, understanding man who simply adores you! He tells you he loves you every day and he buys you gifts – gorgeous dresses, takes you on date nights, spoils you rotten and, the best of all, covers you in prayer every day! He loves to hear your dreams and he pushes you to your dreams and challenges your limits! He loves your cooking and is your best friend. Seems like a dream, right? No, God is faithful!

When God says he has good plans for you (Jeremiah 29:11), he means it! Trust him. He has better plans than you could ever imagine. Oh, I did not mention that so far you have two gorgeous daughters, Thandiwe and Ivanna. That's a story for another day. So my advice for you is this:

Don't panic that you will not meet and marry a good man – focus rather on God's standards of a godly woman. Grow yourself and find your identity in Christ because we attract who we are.

Don't bother looking for affirmation in all the boys who have crushes on you. If they don't love God, they don't even know what love is and how to treat you right.

Focus and study hard. It will pay off! You will earn the gift of hard-earned money when you begin to pay your taxes.

Pray and ask God for real, genuine, godly girlfriends. I know you say girls are too emotional, but emotions are good. Once you know how you feel, that is when you can control your emotions and realize their impact on others. Good friends influence a lot of the decisions you make and the values you hold.

Please stop watching the soaps and living in a fantasy! That stuff is all meant to arouse the wrong feelings at the wrong time. It is based on jealousy, hatred, revenge, and all that is not God. Read 1 Corinthians 13. That is love. You will need to throw out a lot of DVDs and chick flicks as well. They are toxic to your soul. Take a Bible, spend time with Jesus, and be loved and love.

Finally, forgive. Forgive yourself. Forgive those who have wronged you. Forgiveness will free you and help you receive and offer grace.

Love,

Waturi Wamboye (Yes, that's your new name now!)

9

EMOTIONAL PURITY

ABOVE ALL ELSE, GUARD YOUR HEART, FOR EVERYTHING YOU DO FLOWS FROM IT. PROVERBS 4:23

We desire to see young people marry well. One topic that is inevitable to discuss is that of emotional purity. We often speak about sexual integrity at the expense of emotional integrity. When my wife and I were in campus, we had a rule concerning our dating relationship. It was simple: the relationship was exclusive. While it sounds obvious, the lines of exclusivity become really blurry when a member of the opposite sex fits themselves into the equation. It is as if they are squeezing in-between a two-seater couch where you and your boyfriend/girlfriend are seated.

The seat can only accommodate two but there's an "invited" friend who has wedged himself or herself in to participate in your lives. I say invited because one of the partners in the relationship allowed the stranger to sit, or rather, they watched them sit and did nothing. A crowded couch is no fun. Most likely, one original member of the relationship will leave because their partner won't speak up to protect their intimacy in the relationship. Relationships work best when they are exclusive. And for exclusivity to happen, those boundaries need to be drawn clearly and intentionally by both women and men.

For a very long time, I did not know that I was hurting Turi. I didn't necessarily have a best friend of the opposite sex, but I entertained a lot of people on the relationship couch. I was a student leader in campus in charge of student clubs and social activities. Because of that, I was compelled to work very closely with students, especially those interested in student activities – most notably the freshmen. I worked late on reports with them. I sat down with them to design club projects. I personally showed them around school when they wanted to join clubs.

Needless to say, the majority of these were ladies. I developed friendships with some of them, but I did not draw clear boundaries. It would come off as a shock to my girlfriend when these ladies kissed me on the cheek to say thank you or asked me to meet them for lunch after a long morning of work. I was oblivious to the issue. It persisted and I did nothing to stop the pecks, the long hugs, the random lunch meetings, and the hang-out times after class. I was breaching the very rule I created. The relationship was not exclusive.

LACK OF EXCLUSIVITY INVITES DISRESPECT

When you fail to draw boundaries of exclusivity, intruders will fail to respect you and your relationship. Once, while we were dating, Turi and I attended a concert in school. The auditorium was crowded, noisy with blasting music, and there were no empty seats. One pretty girl who was my friend walked up to where I was. She was looking for a seat. She saw me. She was clad in a fitted short dress. She held the hem of her dress, pulled it down a little, walked up to me, and sat on my lap. She did it so naturally and casually; I could hardly believe her audacity. Turi, who was seated next to me, was the object of everyone's vision; they wanted to see her reaction. Everyone there, including the girl seated on my lap, knew that Turi was my girlfriend. I arose from my seat and asked the girl to have my seat instead. I stood during the concert. As I stood, I tried to process what had just happened.

WHEN YOU FAIL TO DRAW BOUNDARIES OF EXCLUSIVITY, INTRUDERS WILL FAIL TO RESPECT YOU AND YOUR RELATIONSHIP.

Later, Turi told me that she was proud of me for not letting that girl sit on my lap. However, I couldn't help but think, "Doesn't this girl respect my relationship?" "Does she not respect me?" In retrospect I saw the kind of friendship I entertained with this girl. I had developed a fondness for her, and she had done the same because I called her a special name. It wasn't anything to be ashamed of, but it created an avenue to have internal jokes and games with her, yet she wasn't my girl. When you playfully call that girl "doll-face", "your twin", "your muffin", etc., and she is not your girlfriend or he is not your boyfriend, you will hurt your partner eventually. And don't be surprised if "doll-face" kisses you openly in the presence of your girlfriend. Don't be surprised when "muffin" asks to take you for dinner and your boyfriend is watching. You asked for the disrespect when you did not make the relationship exclusive. And when it happens, don't blame the intruder. You can't stop birds from flying over your head, but you can stop them from building a nest in your hair.

BE EXCLUSIVE BUT DON'T ACT MARRIED

When I say exclusive, don't get me wrong. Some couples act married when they are not and call it exclusive. That is not exclusivity. Acting married when you are not can ruin great positive respectful friendships with the opposite sex because you constantly feel threatened. A mature mark of a relationship is a healthy relationship with other members of the opposite sex within respectful boundaries. There's a fine line between exclusivity and acting married; that line is called insecurity. You cannot track down every member of the opposite sex and tell them to keep off your man. You will scare everyone off and eventually scare your partner out of the relationship. To avoid the insecurity that manifests itself by acting married when we were not, Turi and I simply agreed that we would not subscribe to marriage behaviour before we got married. Here are a few of the things we avoided to stop acting married:

- We avoided getting involved sexually in any way before marriage.
- We did not sleep over at each other's places.
- We did not hang out in each other's rooms alone.
- We did not handle each other's personal money.
- We did not access each other's personal forms of communication, i.e., mobile phone calls, text messages, emails, social media, etc.
- We avoided exposing our nudity to each other, e.g., swimming when alone. We had friends tag along always.

These may seem like trivial things, but when unmarried folk engage in them, they create a recipe for disaster. When your relationship couch is intruded upon while you act married, you most likely will end up looking like the guilty party when you speak up. Why? Some of the things I mentioned, such as sexual involvement, create infinitely deep bonds between people. When an intruder comes onto the couch, there will be no confronting them without first dealing with your own insecurities. You will panic when he receives a call from that girl. You will be depressed when you see him talking to her. You cannot respond to the exclusivity without addressing your insecurity of losing a bond you should have reserved for a marriage. If you've breached some of those lines, don't be downcast. There is no rulebook that says you cannot have a brand-new start in life!

EXCLUSIVITY CREATES RESPECT

I am forever grateful for a wife like Turi. She gathered courage, bit the bullet, and confronted me squarely about how she felt. When you are exclusive without acting married, you retain a mind of your own concerning things that affect you and you earn the respect of your partner. I respected Turi for the confrontation. I respected her even more when she declared that her sexual expression was for her marital bed and her husband. I respected her more when she chose not to answer my phone even when I wasn't around.

DEALING WITH INSECURITY

Turi and I also drew our security deeply from having a personal relationship with Christ Jesus. She and I knew that even if you don't do all the things I mentioned in the list, you could still act married and be insecure if your identity is in your relationship. We got insecure several times and we chose to deal with it permanently. We chose not to have our relationship define us. Instead, Christ's love for us defined us. We would choose Christ over each other on any day, even today. We cultivated our personal relationships with Christ by living for him; consequently, we pleased each other. Because Christ was first in our priorities, he enabled us to relate well in our other areas. It wasn't perfect though. I grew jealous once in a while. She also grew envious at times, but Christ was the true north we defaulted to every time our insecurity threatened to rise and consume us.

If your exclusivity in your relationship is threatened, confront it gracefully and lovingly. Don't assume it will go away. Don't pretend it does not exist. Don't simmer in anger and silence. Don't assume your partner knows. You have will power; exercise it. Turi's confrontation was clear as day; she wasn't going to share my heart. If the girls on the overcrowded couch did not leave, she wasn't going to stay. Respect your partner for that courage.

There are few things that hurt a human heart more than when love is not reciprocated, especially after you agree mutually on a standard. Before you call a person jealous, hear her or his heart out. I foresaw the possibility of a break-up because I loved the egotistical sound of ladies saying they wished they had a boyfriend like me, because in lust I did not protest the several kisses on the cheek, because in folly I forgot that I loved Turi, because in the pride of life I wanted to be "the man". I bit the dust because all these things I was pursuing and the false front I put up of "we're just friends" were not giving me the satisfaction I hoped they would. It was time to live up to my words. It was time to make the relationship exclusive. I prayed to God to grant me the strength to do so and he did. Making the promise did not make me capable; it made me accountable.

MAKE THE WRONGS RIGHT

I apologized to Turi. I asked the girls not to peck me. I stopped them pecking me if they didn't listen, even if it meant embarrassing them. I avoided sensual hugs. I stopped late-night or intimate chats with the opposite sex. I took Turi out on more dates. I deleted some of the girls' phone numbers. I began to notice Turi's beauty again. Turi and I experienced a renewal in the relationship. I noticed that the girls respected me when I drew the boundaries. They respected Turi more.

Still, no relationship is disrespect-proof. Someone somewhere doesn't care about what you have. Someone somewhere still has the audacity to flirt with your significant other even in your presence. When that happened, Turi and I wouldn't let the offence separate us. We stood together. I wouldn't get angry and ask her why the intruder was calling her on our honeymoon (and he was, by the way). Instead, I became her partner and helped fight the intruder. We fought it together. I picked up her phone on our honeymoon and the not-so-gentleman on the receiving end was surprised that the husband picked up.

Once you say "I do!" you can act married. Those who noticed you didn't act married while you were dating may be shocked that your phone can be picked by your partner. Marriage made our relationship more exclusive, but it didn't stop intruders from trying to squeeze for a place on the two-seater couch. It didn't stop a few girls from getting excited over our special memories more than we did. It didn't stop a few guys from thinking they would get exclusive time with my wife even after we were married. But it stopped them from doing it a second time when we put up a united front and declared the relationship exclusive in speech, conduct, and action. The couch is now a two-seater with only two seated and there is room to stretch; I advise you to make yours the same.

Over the years, we have had several people send emails to us of being in similar relationship dilemmas. Some morph into unimaginable scenarios. One says, "I am in love with two people." Another says, "I love a man but he is married." Another one says he and his best friend's girlfriend are in love. Some have crossed sexual boundaries and live with the repercussions up to date. They seem to all have the same questions when they write:

- She is someone's wife, but I just fell in love and I don't know how it happened. How do I get out of this mess?
- We are not dating but things got awkward between us.
- One day we found ourselves admitting that we liked each other. His girlfriend and my boyfriend don't know.
- He is married but I am always thinking about him.
- I feel we were meant to be, but she knows I have a girlfriend.
- I'm married but I like this other guy.

I am certain there are a variety of diagnoses we can refer to many of the scenarios above. Do these people walk with God? Are they committed? What was the foundation of the relationship? Do they know the meaning of marriage? Do they understand what love truly is? And these are very valid and important questions to answer. However, one of the reasons many scenarios like these are rife in our generation is because people calculate relationships with their IQ while they ought to be calculating it with their EQ (emotional intelligence quotient).

Solomon advised us in Proverbs 4:23, "Above all else, guard your heart, for everything you do flows from it." Many people have not learned the art of guarding their hearts. To put it so crudely, we have a generation of Einsteins in the workplace and in the universities but who pale when it comes to relationships. They score bonuses in the corporate world but are toddlers while handling their wives or girlfriends. They score valedictorian GPAs in their alma maters but are babes when it comes to relating with their husbands or boyfriends.

When a man goes to hang out with one of his "platonic" female friends in her house all alone, the blind see a catch-up session, the wise see a lack of emotional intelligence.

When a lady opens up to her male colleague at work about the troubles in her marriage, the blind see a good friendship, but the wise see a lack of emotional intelligence.

When a man is dating a girl but has a different girl as his "BFF", the blind see a platonic relationship but the wise see a lack of emotional intelligence.

When a girl is dating a guy but spends late nights chatting on WhatsApp with a different guy, the blind see an innocent conversation, the wise see a lack of emotional intelligence.

The dullness of our emotional intelligence is even more shocking when the above scenarios brew discord in our relationships and we lamely defend our tomfoolery with statements like:

- We just had coffee!
- It's not like we slept together!
- I told him I have a boyfriend, but he wouldn't listen.
- It's not my fault that people flirt with me.
- She's going through a rough patch; I was only being there for her.
- Are you jealous?
- There's nothing going on!
- Can't I have friends of the opposite sex?

And when things get out of hand and boundaries are crossed and we hurt our partner, our mouths only show more dullness and little emotional intelligence.

- He makes me feel alive.
- She listens to me; you don't.
- He treats me better that my boyfriend does.
- She is the one meant for me.

Anyone who falls in love with someone else while in a relationship is not a victim, but a perpetrator. Almost without exception, sexual affairs start as emotional affairs. Emotional unfaithfulness is very hurtful, and it can cause as much damage as a sexual affair if your partner finds out. Here are a few tips to help you better yourself for the future and guard your heart.

TAKE RESPONSIBILITY FOR THE EMOTIONAL AFFAIR

The most common excuse that shouts irresponsibility is this one: "I just don't know how it happened!" If you are still self-deceived about this, allow me to unmask you. Get rid of the myth that falling in love is an accident. Unfortunately, that is a trope from Disney and Hollywood. And more unfortunate is that people believe it. You must understand that people don't fall in love by accident.

Falling in love is a result of expended time, conversations, and emotions with someone of the opposite sex. The chemistry between a man and a woman is never accidental. People fall in love by design not by default. The day you accepted to having lunch exclusively, you designed it. The day you decided to walk her home every evening, you designed it. You must take responsibility. Someone may argue and say, "But I truly never intended for this to happen." Very true, but you must realize this: <u>an unintentional commitment to things that do not matter is an intentional lack of commitment to things that do matter.</u>

You have two options: you can make excuses, or you can make progress, but you cannot make both. The man and woman without emotional intelligence see these two scenarios and may say, "Okay, I admit responsibility. Things got awkward and they shouldn't have gone this far. But what is wrong with having lunch? What is wrong with walking home together?" In order to understand the deeper problem, you must grasp the anatomy of an emotional affair.

THE ANATOMY OF AN EMOTIONAL AFFAIR

We have already stated that falling in love is a result of expended time, conversations, and emotions with someone of the opposite sex. I am not saying to never talk or spend time with someone of the opposite sex. I know you are wiser than to think that. However, the key words are *exclusive* and *consistent!* This is the general anatomy. Exclusive and consistent energy spent with someone of the opposite sex will create a connection between the two of you. If this person is not someone you are prepared to spend the rest of your life with, you will break a heart – maybe even yours. But how do I do this when I work with this person? I see them every day. I can't avoid them! The answer is to create boundaries. You can't stop birds from flying over you, but you can stop them from creating a nest on your head. One boundary you should have is with regard to depth of conversations.

In her book, *I Don't Get You: A Guide to Healthy Conversations*, Sherry Graf lists five levels of conversation to help us understand the boundaries we need to draw.[17]

Level one conversations start with biodata: what your name is, where you live, where you went to school, etc. This is basic information to which a stranger in the bus can be privy. Anybody who knows this isn't really special to you, they have simply interacted with you on base-level. They are on level one.

Level two conversations dwell on general personal experiences. This could include your faith journey. How was your childhood and upbringing? The best way to guard your heart in this area is to observe the context. Sharing on this level in a group may be harmless, but in a one-on-one with the opposite sex it may lead to emotional entanglements as you may easily jump into deeper levels, too fast and too soon. Sherry's advice is to stick to the

THE LEVEL OF INTIMACY SHOULD DETERMINE THE LEVEL OF COMMUNICATION.

basic facts of your testimony without going too deep. Look at the other levels to understand what too deep means.

Level three conversations involve your dreams and passions. This involves talking about the things that excite you and make you want to get up each day. They are at times linked to your career and your purpose. This is an area that makes us develop interest in someone, especially if he or she shares our dreams and aspirations.

Level four conversation is when you talk about your fears. This is the kind of conversation that occurs in hushed tones. It could be the fear of getting married because you saw your parents fight a lot. It could be the fear of not getting married because you feel you wasted some time in your twenties. It could be the fear of dying because your faith is shaky. It could be the fear of disappointing yourself after so many mistakes in life. Sharing your fears creates emotional ties faster than you can say "oops"! Proverbs 4:23 says, "Above all else, guard your heart, for everything you do flows from it." One reason emotional affairs ravage men and women is because people have exclusive and consistent conversations about their deep personal fears. When the other person empathizes, you connect emotionally. When they reciprocate their fears, too, you become more than friends. People who call themselves best friends have these conversations freely. If you must have these conversations with a best friend, let them be of the same sex. Otherwise, an emotional entanglement with someone of the opposite sex is imminent.

The fifth level of conversation (which is also the most intimate) is when you talk about your deepest hurts. If you get to this level comfortably with someone of the opposite sex, you will get deeply tied emotionally. This is emotional treasure. What often happens with a confession of deepest hurts is a craving for comfort. This comfort is often manifested in touch – a hug, a back rub, a side-hug, a hand clasp, etc. It seems natural but it sets a precedent for more such conversations and eventually for unwanted inappropriateness. Deep hurts such as rape, defilement as a child, a cheating ex, death of a loved one, violence and torture, abuse that left you wounded, father wounds, etc. are emotional deposits of gold. Invest them with the wrong person and you set yourself up for failure.

So how far should we go in the conversation levels? Sherry states that the level of intimacy should determine the level of communication.[18] To avoid getting legalistic, she gives this brilliant advice. We must decide prayerfully. And if in doubt, it is best to err on the side of caution. I strongly advise being particularly careful not to venture into levels four and five carelessly, especially with someone of the opposite sex who isn't your significant other. Even with your significant other, it is wise to approach the matter carefully. I would also caution being wise concerning levels one to three. Sherry emphasizes that the content and context of the conversations are what determine intimacy.[19] Having a simple conversation on a public queue may do no harm. But having it in a secluded room, face to face, will start building those emotional ties. I believe with regard to levels one to three we must primarily guard our hearts with regards to context. With levels four to five, we must primarily guard our hearts with regards to content. With levels four and five, if we disregard both context and content we get into the worst emotional situations.

A second boundary you should have is that of spending exclusive and consistent time together. Exclusive and consistent time together creates familiarity. Consider what Elizabeth Elliot writes in her book *Passion and Purity*. This applies to women, specifically:

> Unless a man is prepared to ask a woman to be his wife, what right has he to claim her exclusive attention? Unless she has been asked to marry him, why would a sensible woman promise any man her exclusive attention? If, when the time has come for a commitment, he is not man enough to ask her to marry him, she should give him no reason to presume that she belongs to him.[20]

We can transliterate Elliot's words for the men too.
Here goes:

> Unless a woman is prepared to be a man's wife, what right has she to claim his exclusive attention? Unless she desires to marry him, why would a sensible man promise any woman his exclusive attention? If, when the time has come for a commitment, she is not woman enough to accept his proposal, he should give her no reason to presume that he belongs to her.

Exclusive and consistent time alone with someone of the opposite sex that you will not spend the rest of your life with bespeaks a lack of emotional intelligence and sets a stage for emotional infidelity. Well, what if I have gone too far, I have crossed boundaries, and I want to stop? What do I do?

To extinguish the fire of the emotional affair, you need to get rid of the fuel. You must look where you slipped, not where you fell. If you fell in love because of exclusive and consistent time and conversations, you need to establish that and, out of character and respect for your relationship, stop it. Stop the chatting. Stop the lunches. Stop the late hours together. These things seem harmless at the onset, but if you are in a relationship with someone already, you begin to disdain your partner and value the one you are having an emotional thrill with. The person you are wrongly connecting with emotionally may ask why you cut links. Don't lie about it. Don't say you got busy or you have to run home early. Let them know that you crossed boundaries with them that you ought to have observed.

If you have a spouse or a significant other, let the other person know that you are in a relationship, and that whatever is going on is wrong for your relationship. You must be clear about the boundary. A boundary that is not verbally stated does not exist. State it clearly and respectfully. Now, when you get rid of the fuel of the emotional affair, you may be surprised that your feelings still linger. It's normal. You have a heart, not a computer chip for programming.

You also need to reconnect emotionally with your spouse/ significant other. In this period of emotional distance, your spouse/significant other has almost become a stranger. You must reconnect even though your feelings do not say so. A relationship must be fought for, even when the enemy is yourself. One real test of maturity in a relationship is having the capacity to commit to the relationship when the feelings are absent. If you are unmarried, you will need this ethic to keep your marriage in the future. The world says follow your heart. That is lousy advice. Follow your convictions. The Scriptures tell us in Jeremiah 17:9, "The heart is deceitful above all things and beyond cure. Who can understand it?"

Your heart wants to leave your partner and follow the temporal thrill of this new flame. It is a false and fleeting high. Reconnect. To be practical, go on more dates. For the married and only for the married, have more sexual intimacy. Soon, you will lose the passion for the wrong one and gain a new flame for the right one. Even Solomon, the wisest that lived (apart from Christ) said in Proverbs 30:19 that one of the four strangest things he could not understand was how a man and a woman connect. The wisest could have fallen for it. Let us be careful.

10

SEXUAL PURITY

**BUT AMONG YOU THERE MUST NOT BE EVEN
A HINT OF SEXUAL IMMORALITY.
EPHESIANS 5:3A**

The world has many false ideas about the Christian and sex. Some Christians have these untrue notions embedded in their belief system as well. Very often I hear men and women state fallacies about how believers perceive sex. I am often tempted to roll my eyes, but for today I will write about it. The standard for the believer is to reserve sex for the marriage bed between one man and one woman. While this may seem an archaic move for many contemporary people, we must understand everything the Bible says, beyond the simple truth of 1 Thessalonians 4:3, "It is God's will that you should be sanctified: that you should avoid sexual immorality." Let's look at some popular myths about sex.

1. SEX IS A DIRTY THING AND THE BIBLE IS ANTI-SEX

We must start by qualifying that sex is a great thing according to the Scriptures. It is possibly the greatest ecstasy that your physical body will experience on this planet before you die. There are Scriptures in the Bible that if read aloud would make any liberal blush. For example, Proverbs 5:18-19 speaks to the young man who has just tied the knot. It says to him concerning sex, "May your fountain be blessed, and may you rejoice in the wife of your youth. A loving doe, a graceful deer – may her breasts satisfy you always, may you ever be intoxicated with her love." Yes, those are literal breasts. Solomon is not talking about spiritual breasts that give spiritual milk for the edification of the church. No. He is talking of an exhilarating and erotic experience that a man ought to share with his woman once they are married and it is not pornographic or dirty. And the Bible is clear that women enjoy the sexual experience too. The Shulammite woman in Song of Songs 1:2 says this concerning her husband, Solomon, "Let him kiss me with the kisses of his mouth – for your love is more delightful than wine." Yes, it is a lover's kiss that has the full endorsement of the Godhead. In Genesis 26:8 King Abimelek is looking out the window of a house and sees a private moment between Isaac and his wife Rebekah. They are possibly having foreplay as it is written that he is caressing her. Well, what does all this teach us?

> **THE BIBLE IS NOT ANTI-SEX. THE BIBLE IS FOR SEX. OUR HOLY BOOK BEGINS WITH TWO NAKED PEOPLE IN A GARDEN, FOR CRYING OUT LOUD!**

One, that married people should buy curtains for their bedrooms. But also, two, that the Bible is not anti-sex. The Bible is for sex. Our holy book begins with two naked people in a garden, for crying out loud! Sex is not a thing of the world that God borrowed and decided to customize it for believers. It was his creation right from the onset in Genesis 1:28. Adam and Eve were commanded to fill the world. How in the world were they going to do that? Cell division? I think not. It was through the beautiful act of sex. You must know this because one of the oldest lies of the enemy is that God wants to curtail your freedom and joy, especially sexually.

There are sexual sins that the Lord openly repudiates because they pervert the beauty of his creation. However, many people only know what God is against; they forget what he is for. And he is for sex. The Word of God says that God's plans for you are good, pleasing, and perfect (Romans 12:2). All his plans, including his sexual plan for you.

2. SEX IS JUST A PHYSICAL APPETITE

Unlike eating or drinking, fulfilling our sexual desires has profound impacts on our souls. Sex is not like any other appetite. Whilst analogies can be made to understand how it works, no comparison to any other physical appetite can capture its profound impact on our thoughts, emotions, and will power. When you are hungry and you are next to a restaurant, you take time off to satisfy your hunger. As you do so, guilt does not well up your soul that you are cheating on the other restaurant in your neighbourhood. But sex does that. When you quench your thirst with a bottle of water, you don't end up fantasising about that bottle of water for the next few weeks. You don't get sleepless nights imagining someone else is using that bottle. But sex does that. Why?

Because sex is not just a flesh-on-flesh experience. It is deeper than that. It involves your soul. Your soul is your mind, your will, and your emotions. Countless people today are facing depression from rejection by sexual partners. An ordinary appetite cannot do that to you. But sex can. This is something that the Bible has clearly taught when it says you become one with the person you join yourself to sexually (1 Corinthians 6:16).

That oneness is more than physical oneness. It involves more than your physical body. The world only imagines the most dangerous thing about fornication to be unwanted babies and possible STI's. We may avoid the physical ramifications, but we must understand that there is no condom for the soul. Your soul is entangled with someone at the deepest level of your being when you sexually join yourself to her or him. The Bible says you become one. And that is why the ideas of one-night stands and sex without feelings are the peak of self-deception.

Sweeping the dirt under the carpet doesn't make the room clean; it only makes you in denial and out of touch with your soul. Your soul was made to be truly and fully satisfied only by its Creator. Sex is but a false god that promises that satisfaction. The emptiness even after the "appetite" is fulfilled speaks of a deeper longing within us. We are not complete without the lover of our souls – and it isn't sex or money or romance or success. It is God. Our souls were made for him. We need the giver of the gifts more than the gifts.

3. SEX BEFORE MARRIAGE WILL HELP ME SELECT THE PERFECT MATE

For starters, fornication cannot prepare you for marriage. If anything, sin makes you less prepared for marriage. Our generation strongly believes in the test-and-drive idea as far as sex is concerned. Many Christians in campus often tell us of how all their friends do not understand how they choose to wait for sex until marriage. In their defence, they say you do not want to end up with a lousy bedmate. The solution is to test-drive (through intercourse) in order to find a sexually compatible mate. And often we ask them, "What happens to the candidates who do not pass the compatibility test?" While many refuse to answer, we get the simple and direct answer; get rid of them and look for another one. The heart of this notion is to have a glimpse of what kind of marriage you will have. The plan is to have a sneak peek just like a movie trailer. Using sex as a mate selection tool has downsides.

Firstly, unsuitable sexual candidates are changed like soiled diapers and thrown away. The less an ex with whom you had a sexual encounter shows up in your present life, the better it is for you. Our generation breaks up and is dating tomorrow at lunch hour. The ex is left high and dry. With such treatment, we reduce their inherent human value. In fact, many exes become sworn enemies. People have hearts that break, not engines that break down. We cannot test-drive a soul because it is more complex and infinitely more valuable than a simple vehicle. The idea of test driving reduces a human being to an object. This is the heart behind pornography and the rape culture in many societies today. To consent to the test-and-drive idea is to further this agenda. Sexual objectification is one of the biggest vices we are facing in society.

Secondly, the meaning and beauty of sex is reduced to an audition or an interview. God created sex for the man and the woman to complement a marriage union. But we now use it to compete towards a marriage union. To the world, sex is an auditioning process; if you fail, you won't get cast. If you pass, you get the role. And even if you get casted, you

PEOPLE HAVE HEARTS THAT BREAK, NOT ENGINES THAT BREAK DOWN.

must master all your lines and keep the performance on the up and up because you could be replaced with an understudy who seems to have more potential. If you slip up or do not show up for practice, the play will continue and they will find another actor/actress. With this mindset, several young people in our generation rate the health of a relationship based on the frequency and ecstasy of sex. This is impractical.

It is impractical because you are basically marrying for sex under that ideology. Yet sex is a very small part of marriage. Anecdotal and empirical evidence suggests that an average married couple can have sex twice a week. When you get married you will not have sex every week. You can even go a fortnight without it. And no, you will not fall sick. Nobody has actually ever died from not having sex. But many have died from having it illegitimately. But let us assume you have sex twice a week, every week.

Some human sexuality studies and anecdotal evidence tell us that the average sexual encounter lasts 10 minutes. Ten minutes, twice a week is 20 minutes. In a week there are 10,080 minutes. In an ideal (and grossly exaggerated) world, you will spend every week of your life having sex. In each week you will clock 20 minutes out of a whopping 10,080 minutes of your life. Even if we assume this rate to be constant (and it is not), 20 minutes only accounts for 0.198 per cent. Let us round it off to 0.2 per cent just to encourage a few. In essence, you will spend 0.2 per cent of your time on Earth having sex if your life is constant and your weeks the very same. What in the world will you do with 99.8 per cent of your life? Even if you boast of your legendary virility to have sex every day of the week, you are limited to 70 minutes in a week. The calculation still puts it way below 1 per cent. This is the point: there is more to life than sex. You cannot marry for sex.

To use sex as an audition for a life partner is to trade 99.8 per cent of your life for a 0.2 per cent experience.

You may marry the sexual fantasy of your desires but remember that sex does not raise children or pay the bills or maintain a marriage. If good looks and sex could maintain a marriage, all the Hollywood marriages would be our examples to follow. But they are not. They are always breaking.

We must consider better qualifications for a life partner. We must be concerned about their character more than their prowess in bed. What benefit is there to get the sexual idol of your heart but constantly deal with bad temper, a nagging attitude, an unteachable know-it-all spirit, or an unfaithful character? Sex is important, but there are a myriad of issues to consider. And for that reason, to test-drive sex in the name of selecting a life partner is highly impractical.

It is also impractical because sex ceases to be an act of making love and it becomes a bedroom theatrical performance act. The world's assumption is the more mind-blowing the sex, the better the relationship will be. Nothing could be further from the truth. You must understand that good sex does not make a good marriage. It is the other way round. A good marriage produces great sex. Sex does not regulate the temperature of a marriage. A marriage regulates the temperature of sex.

The world thinks that the way to fix a dying and boring marriage is to spice up the bedroom. They are wrong. The truth is that the way to fix a dying and boring sex life is to fix your marriage. You experience greater sexual satisfaction if you and your spouse are kind to each other, if you are patient with each other, if you are considerate to each other. Sex that blows your mind is rooted in character that melts your heart. Great sex is a by-product of a working marriage. It is not the producer of great marriages. The world has put the cart before the horse because they do not understand that sex is a gift for marriage not an audition for dating.

4. I WILL FINALLY FIND THAT ONE SEXUALLY COMPATIBLE MATE

The idea of finding the one perfect mate who will envelop us with love and affection is really selfish. Remember Keller's quote: "It is possible to feel you are 'madly in love' with someone, when it is really just an attraction to someone who can meet your needs and address the insecurities and doubts you have about yourself. In that kind of relationship, you will demand and control rather than serve and give."[21] And as a result everyone gets into a relationship innately thinking, "What about me, me, me?" The trouble with this is that you will spend your whole life looking for the perfect sex mate and even if you find the ultimate, the flesh will always show you the new kid on the block. You will never settle and you will never be satisfied because of selfishness. You may marry your sexual fantasy, but you will never be content. "The heart is deceitful above all things and beyond cure" (Jeremiah 17:9), and you will never be satisfied.

Even after you get married, your heart will lie to you that there is a better sexual experience out there. In God's economy, your neighbour comes before you, even in the sexual act. Sex for the believer is an act of giving not receiving. You mutually enter in to **GOD'S STANDARD IS LOVE; THE WORLD'S STANDARD IS LUST.** satisfy one another not to outdo one another. In God's will, the pressure is off and the fear of performance turns to passionate service because God's gifts are not expressed in fear. God's standard is love; the world's standard is lust. My friend, Winnie Waruguru makes it very clear:

Lust wants the here and now because it burns up and out like a thirsty fire; Love wants the forever and always because it shines on and on like the sure sun. Love is patient.

Lust tells me: hurry up, before anyone knows. Love tells me: wait until everyone knows. Love is patient.

Lust strips my body and soul naked and leaves me out in the cold; Love covers me up and keeps me warm. It awaits the time it will strip me, only to shelter me in its assuredness. Love is patient.

Lust overdraws on an uncertain tomorrow to pay for unnecessary expenses today; Love invests in a sure tomorrow while avoiding unnecessary expenses today. Love is patient.

Lust stages a coup on my heart, threatened; because it knows it is not its rightful ruler; Love waits patiently as a Crown Prince waits for years, confident because it knows it's the rightful heir. Love is patient.

(A poem by Winnie Waruguru).[22]

5. PREMARITAL SEX IS PRACTICE FOR MARRIAGE SEX

The world makes a gross assumption that this planet is divided into two people: good in bed and bad in bed. They imagine that the world has tantalising sexual beasts who will give you apocalyptic sex. On the other hand, it also has weak dwarves with little prowess. And their end game is to warn you lest you end up with a dwarf. They caution you to better test-drive before you ride so that you can locate a beast that will ravish you until you are weak with pleasure.

That is just not true. Sex is not a marathon with few people who are very good at it. Sex is more like taking a walk with your lover. There is no competition to win because you are on the same team. You take a stroll through the park, hand in hand. You run a little in the meadow. You tickle one another as you sit on the bench. You take his jacket when it feels cold. You run down the hill. You wait for the rain to pass as you stand under a shelter. You splash the water on each other. And you eventually get home to a warm fire. This is the kind of sex that doesn't need a beast; it needs a friend.

In marriage, sex with a friend is better than sex with a beast. Sex with a beast is the force behind pornography. Sex with a friend is the lasting romance behind a godly marriage. Sex is a not a marathon because marriage is not a competition. Wait patiently. The fermentation of your feelings right now is a test of patience and an establishing of your character and you will not regret it in the marriage bed.

Waiting for sex until marriage does not disqualify you in any way because sex is something you learn as you go. Good sex is like good wine; it gets better with time provided it stays in the same bottle. Your bottle is your marriage. It gets better with time as you relate with your spouse. Mix it with new wines and you ruin it. Share your sexual energy with anyone apart from your spouse and the wine that took years to mature can be cheapened to local grape juice. One reason sex inside marriage gets better with time is because you are not competing with your spouse to outperform one another. You are giving yourselves to each other in a patient and kind way – a 1 Corinthians 13 way.

In their book, *Our Sexuality*, Robert L. Crooks and Karla Baur cite a work by the National Health and Social Life Survey (NHSLS) concerning sexual enjoyment. They explicitly show that married people have greater sexual satisfaction than dating and cohabiting couples. The women specifically experience much greater sexual satisfaction through having more orgasms than their counterparts having sex outside of marriage. Crooks and Baur go on to state that sexual interest and intensity is maintained in long-term relationships.[23]

WHY PURSUE PURITY?

The message of purity is primarily for the believer, not the unbeliever. Unbelievers have bigger problems than purity; they have an eternity conundrum to sort out first. We must pursue purity for the sake of the gospel. The gospel is not a pile-up of more morality. It is to turn from sin and follow Jesus. The gospel wants spiritual fruit and not religious nuts. In the faith, you realize that the answer to broken relationships is forgiveness and reconciliation. I have talked to many unbelieving friends who solve broken relationships with sex. When things go wrong in a relationship, they decide, "Let's have sex. It will make us feel good and produce good feelings; then we will deal with the issue."

But the problem is that even after sex, the issues have not gone away. In God's economy, when a marriage faces trouble, the couple focuses on the issue, resolves it, and has sex as the celebration. After the sex act, they are closer to one another. The pursuit of purity enables the gospel to deal with our sin without hoping an alternative deed will wipe it away. We must also pursue purity to experience the blessings of God and realize that God heals and forgives all sexual shortcomings.

You must consider that Jesus demonstrated his love for you, and to that end he died. You can therefore live for him and die to self.

We must also be careful about whom we associate with. The Bible says that "bad company corrupts good character" (1 Corinthians 15:33) and that a companion of fools will suffer harm (Proverbs 13:20). Our pursuit is only as good as our partners. A believer who  desires to make it to the altar pure must know that friendships influence. When your supposed friends say statements such as "all men must cheat" or "all women are loose", and you yield to their deceit without debate, you allow the words to take root in your belief system. Words, just like seeds, need to remain undisturbed in their planted places in order for them to take root. We often ignore the power of silence.

The Word of God tells us in 2 Corinthians 10:3-5 that the deceitful words must be demolished by the Word of God. The Word of God is designed to take captive every idea and argument that raises itself above the truth. Your silence will make the deceit more irresistible the next time it is voiced. And in no time, you will adopt this falsehood as truth and even become an advocate and champion for it. And even without experiencing it, you will nod your head when it is said that all men must cheat. What you believe results in how you live; consequently, your attempts and chances at relationships with faithful men become as rare as rearing unicorns.

So speak against the lies you hear. Even if your counter argument lacks the fortitude, coherence, and wit to prove the truth, challenge deception. At best you will stop a false belief and negative attitude from germinating in your heart and in the hearts of your hearers. At worst, you will be better prepared to answer your opponents next time by examining what you lack in your present argument. And finally, pray for wisdom to know if the argument at hand is one that profits nothing and is better to be ignored as Paul the apostle taught.

But is sexual purity really possible? Is it practical? For the follower of Jesus, yes, it is. You must realize that God gives everyone the ability to fulfil his commands. "In fact, this is love for God: to keep his commands. And his commands are not burdensome." (1 John 5:3). The Bible further says that all you need to live a godly life you already have: "His divine power has given us everything we need for a godly life through our knowledge of him who called us by his own glory and goodness." (2 Peter 1:3). That means that you are equipped to wait. You must note that 2 Peter says that we are equipped to wait through our knowledge of him, not through our effort, but through our knowledge of him (Jesus).

The more you know the Lord Jesus, the more equipped you are to wait and live a life pleasing to him. The Swahili people say, "*Dawa ya moto ni moto.*" (The remedy for fire is fire.) While it is not a biblical statement, the principle is true. The knowledge of Jesus will give you a bigger passion in your soul. The fire of knowing Jesus will always be greater than every sexual temptation you face. Sexual desire is a good thing given to us by God. But remember that a flame in the fireplace warms a house while a flame outside the fireplace burns the house down.

OUR ULTIMATE GIFT AS BELIEVERS IS NOT "I DO" BUT "WELL DONE!"

Jesus is the passion that contains the flame within the fireplace. Jesus is the reason we wait until marriage – not STIs, not unwanted pregnancies, but Jesus!

He is the one that ensures the flame warms the house and does not destroy it. The enemy will lie to you that Jesus wants to douse the flame with a bucket of cold water. That is not true. He wants to stoke the fire. He wants to add the wood to it. He wants it to keep burning in your marriage. He wants you to be enraptured by it and taste a glimpse of his holiness. He wants it to warm the house and not burn it down.

We ought to recall that we are saved by grace through faith that is not from our effort. If I truly understand what Jesus did on that cross for me, then there really is nothing he cannot ask of me. And if he asks for my sexual purity, then his sacrifice for me melts my heart in obedience to him. Sexual purity becomes a joy to live and not a struggle to endure. If I disregard his request for my sexual purity then I only prove two things: that he is not the Lord of my life, and that the gospel may have not really changed me. And if that is true, it is difficult to know if you belong to him or not. Did you come to Christ to serve God or for God to serve you?

Christ Jesus is the ultimate incentive to wait for sex until marriage. And when you grasp that, it melts your heart to wait; it does not scare you with statistics on disease. When you grasp that, it stops you from asking questions such as, "How far is too far?" Your concern ceases to be, "How close can I get to the sin boundary?" Your concern becomes, "How much can I know Christ?" Those are two different directions. The first is headed towards the sin. The latter is a pursuit of righteousness – fleeing from sin (2 Timothy 2:22). When you delight in God, you gain the grace to resist sin. Christ will uphold all believers who seek purity with all their heart even in the midst of a perverse generation. Keep your eyes on Jesus even as you patiently wait for marriage because our ultimate gift as believers is not "I do" but "Well done!" May you be a good and faithful servant with your sexuality.

11

A LETTER FROM LUST TO A MAN

IT IS GOD'S WILL THAT YOU SHOULD BE SANCTIFIED: THAT YOU SHOULD AVOID SEXUAL IMMORALITY. 1 THESSALONIANS 4:3

I have written two books on the subject of sexual purity. The first is *Lust and the City*.[24] The second is *Holy Joe*. However, I wanted to emphasize that purity is more important than we think. I am convinced that sexual sin, more than any other, has the potential to kill the potential of marrying well. The men especially need to be extra careful. They are the vision-bearers of the marriage. If the enemy can emasculate the man, he will discourage the woman and then break the family. So I dedicate this chapter to men specifically, though women can benefit from it as well. Men need to know that lust will stab them at the heart.

Whilst many vices bring down a man, I believe none aims for his heart more than that of sexual lust. It fascinates him, then assassinates him. It thrills him, then kills him; excites him, then executes him; electrifies him, then electrocutes him. Lust arouses him, then roasts him; inflates him, then deflates him; balloons him, then bursts him. It charms him, then curses him.

The forbidden woman can enchant him to believe the pleasure will last forever. Mainstream entertainment has fooled the man into neglecting his God-given masculinity and trading it for fantasy. Pornography has bewitched him and set him on a false course with false fire only to chase the wind. But when the day is over, the man is falling down the cliff without a chute; he strikes the ground and his soul is writhing in a blood pool of regret. He looks okay on the outside but is dying on the inside. And when he revives enough to get back up, he runs up the same cliff, believing the same old lie, deceiving and being deceived, and off the cliff he goes again. When a man is a slave to sexual lust, he loses power and the biggest loser is his relationships, especially the one with the woman he loves. We need men to reclaim their passion, purpose, and power. I pray that it will inspire you to protect your vision. This is a letter from demonic lust to a man:

FROM DEMONIC LUST

Hello there fool,

Yes, that's right, my lustful, demonized, and desperate fool. That's what you are, no? Not just a fool, what's most important is that you are *my* fool. How did it go today with your so-called "purity journey"? Did you watch that porno again? Wait, don't tell me! You fell again. Hahahaha! I knew you couldn't do it. You're weak. You're pathetic. You're a fool. You amuse me, fool. I think I learn from your mistakes more than you do.

I know your patterns. You tell yourself you won't do it. You go near the door of my house. You hope I won't come out. And when I do, *wham*! I always get you by the jugular! You feel the poisonous, lustful venom stream through your veins. You like the feeling but it's killing you. Hahaha! You pray to the Maker vowing to never repeat it, but I know you will always be back. You can't resist me. Admit it. I'm the kryptonite that you adore. The Achilles heel that you worship. The Delilah to your strength. And yet you can't admit that you are addicted. That's okay. I like you in self-deception mode. You are more fun that way than when you are treating me like a cancer.

There are days you grow a backbone and call me filthy names like *sin*. I wonder who taught you such bad words. Was it your pastor? I hope not, because I got him, too, just like I got you. The funny thing is that you run to me when you are stressed yet you loathe me after we are done. Ha! Truly, you know you are addicted when you seek solace in the very thing that brings you grief.

Anyway, I hear you are now into masturbating and have convinced yourself that since certain animals do it, too, you must be fine. Terrific! Just terrific! You have seen yourself as the beast I deem you to be, my little, beastly, addicted fool. I need you to see yourself as an evolved Zinjanthropus as opposed to one made in the image of the Maker. This way you will compare yourself to lower beings such as penguins. This way you live for no higher power. You just render yourself to my lustful waves of death, hoping to evolve out of your addiction. By the way, I love how your life is falling apart even when I'm not around. Looks like I will get my hell bonus early this century! Hahaha! You are your own self-destructing bomb. I'm glad I'm only doing backup duty. I got a report from a familiar spirit that you have accepted this addiction as a gene problem. Like I said, I love you in self-deception mode.

Between high Heaven and hellish Hades, the only gene you have that I know is a sinful gene from your father, Adam – bless his rebellious soul. And now that we have established the debacle of your sexual failure, I hope you're not thinking of leaving. We have plans for you straight from the abyss. We are pleased to hear that you have already implemented our first plan; you are afraid of making purity decisions in advance because you fear you will break them. Excellent! That's my fool of a boy! That's right where I want you – in self-doubt.

You probably do it because you think you will win this battle by your own strength. As long as you believe that, you will never decide in advance to **YOU THINK YOU WILL WIN THIS BATTLE BY YOUR OWN STRENGTH.** do the right thing and you will never have the power to overcome when the rubber meets the road. Hahaha! You amuse me, fool. I love your fear. You have every right to fear. Because once I am done with you, I'm coming for your woman. I will break her heart so badly that she will hate men because of you. She will hate the idea of marrying a man. You will seal the father wounds she has harboured all her youth. I loved her father, by the way. I've commissioned him as a key sponsor, a sugar daddy, to some university slay queens. He's doing a good job and your woman hates him for it. Maybe you are right, fool. Maybe you don't deserve a good woman like her. She deserves a better man, a pure man. But be sure that after your break-up or divorce, I will go after that pure man as soon as I am done chewing you to smithereens.

You see, my strategy is simple, fool: emasculate the man, discourage the woman, and break the family. In that specific order. Pretty genius, huh? Unlike you, I have a plan to help me succeed. You on the other hand, just wake up each morning and hope that things will align in your favour on that day. What a joke! You really think this is a phase in your life. I'm glad your sensual friends from church call the idea of a godly plan legalistic. And you are surprised when you keep visiting my lucrative porn sites. All the while, you are using your cash to fill the pockets of my agents. That's why I love you, fool; you're my cash-cow and I will milk you dry. Wait, scratch that; I hate you! I hate you so much that I am determined to kill you if I can. But don't worry. I won't do it at once. I'm not that gracious. Yours must be a slow, painful death. It must happen bit by bit, methodically and surgically, one lustful failure at a time, all building up to one grand embarrassing moral crash.

> **MY STRATEGY IS SIMPLE, FOOL: EMASCULATE THE MAN, DISCOURAGE THE WOMAN, AND BREAK THE FAMILY.**

Every possible moment of your day must be invested in lust for me to succeed. I will trap you in your workplace. I will trap you in your gym. I will trap you with the sight of all these girls on the street. Your neck will rupture as you keep turning your head to take in their youthful forms with drooling lust. And as long as I can make you think that the problem is their tight dressing and their short skirts, my killing process is effective. Keep believing that your core lust problem comes from outside of you. And when you start lusting on the ones dressed modestly, I'll be sure to convince you that they were sexually suggestive in their gait or batting of the eye.

See, fool, I need you to blame! Blame the billboards. Blame the lustful photos on your Instagram and social media pages. Blame the government. Blame the girl child empowerment. Blame the feminist. Blame your parents. Blame the movies and series you watch! And I hope you don't plan to stop your binge-watching spree. I need it to convince you that a woman must have ridiculous sexual appeal in order to be beautiful. I need you to hate the sight of your own woman and desire that of the woman you don't have. I need you to blame anyone, everyone, you fool. Blame! Blame! Blame! Blame everyone for your struggle but yourself. Blame the guy that sent you the porn link. Blame your traumatic childhood. Because as long as you blame, you're my fool.

Even better, as long as you blame you can't pray. And this works to my advantage. And if you ever do start praying with your self-justifying attitude, it will be the putrid kind of self-righteous prayer that Hell hallows. Go for it! Anyway, that's enough to do with prayer. I dare not indulge you on the power of this nuke. It has left me with serious war scars from the heavenly host. If you must pray, I will be sure to allow it as long as it has you at the centre focus, and not the Maker, in heavenly, heretical humility.

The idea of you humbling yourself and taking responsibility for your struggle makes me sick, fool. You hear that? Sick to the stomach. Inasmuch as I like to see you down, I can't handle this wilful self-abasement of admitting fault. It makes you focus on the Maker and I can't have that. You are my fool. You hear that? MY FOOL! If you want to abase yourself, I've got the right antidote for you. Let's just take the enthusiasm off your self-righteous justification. Let's turn it into self-pity. It looks like humility, but it still has yourself at the centre of focus. It's a form of godliness that lacks the power.

This pride thing is flexible, fool. But that's for me to know and for you to never find out, filthy scum. Confession is for those fanatics who are so weak that they need help from their Creator. While it's difficult to get my hands on them, I can assure you I will never let go of you. My hands are wrung so perfectly around your pathetic, famished soul, the idea of confession will always scare you with thoughts of judgement and shame. I've figured you, fool. I've figured you good! And don't think I'm leaving your job out of this. I hope to destroy your career with this addiction. I have a number of strategies. I may execute this at the height of your woman's frustration with your relationship.

Your woman is not daft as you think. She knows your web browsers are always cleared and your money is frequently disappearing. She already suspects what's going on. Double tragedy gives me utter pleasure. Your demise is my satisfaction, fool. Or maybe . . . maybe . . . maybe I won't ruin your job. Maybe I will let you have a successful career so that you think it compensates for your moral failure. Yes, yes, that's better, don't you think? I'll distract your attention from your addiction with a salary increase, a bonus or even an employee of the year award. You'll be spick and span on the outside but rotting on the inside. Oh, how they will utter glorious lies at your funeral! He was a good man! He loved God! He must be in a good place! Hahaha! Oh, I'm a genius!

By the way, I hear that your friend Melvin got free from one of my traps. It's a pity because he was this close to cheating on his wife. And by "this close" I mean today was the day! Wretched fool escaped my cage. But I will assign a new demon to him to assess his short-lived victory. It will be hard since he converted to the light when he got born again. But it's no biggie. If I couldn't stop him from becoming a genuine Christian, I can work to make him an ineffective believer. Always doubting his salvation and keeping him in infancy with politically correct theology.

Do you fancy to know how he became my toy before all this? You see we study our patients long and hard before we execute. We know their every move. With miserable Melvin, we started him off at these innocent massage parlours. But his heart was already deceitful and desperately wicked. He fooled himself that he was going to ease his muscles.

But we knew the truth. The lustful happy ending he received on one massage session triggered our official entry. We perched on him a masturbating spirit. He didn't see it coming. And just like you, fool, he was powerless against the slightest sexual titillation. Even the mannequins were stumbling blocks! Can you believe it? The mannequins! He masturbated at every opportune moment. Even during toilet breaks in those work conferences, he indulged in hedonistic self-pleasure. Ha! Self-control is not for fickle-minded fools.

That's why I had to variate his lustful investments. He proceeded to establish inappropriate relationships with his workmates. One of those new colleagues alerted HR. But thankfully he wasn't fired. We directed his focus from real women to the naked, virtual ones on Google. But the genesis of his struggle did not begin with these obviously sinful, happy-ending, body massages. They began with his friends. They were not sinful friends per se, but they were just the right tools I needed. You know, the passive friends who don't encourage you to solicit a call girl but neither do they push you towards righteousness. Perfect allies of Hades!

You see, fool, I don't need to use evil tools to bring you down. I can merely use good things that are not necessarily God things. Good and seemingly harmless entertainment with a few seconds of nudity. Good and harmless music with just a tinge of sensuality. And since Melvin believed the lie that he was a good person, he was ripe for my plucking. It was going so well; it's a pity he didn't cheat on his wife. It would have been a steamy affair with poor Nancy. She was the only work colleague that entertained his lustful flirtations. She was so distressed by her husband's alcoholism (thanks to our competent substance-addiction department), she just wanted a man to find her beautiful. Melvin and Nancy would have had apocalyptic passion, I promise you. Perhaps three months long, two weeks brief at best, it would have been steamy all the same.

If he held on, I would have delivered him three months of his pathetic, nothing-like-the-real version of heaven. And if he was willing to stop going to that Christian fellowship, I would have made it a year with Nancy. Our contracts can even stretch to two years of secrecy and carnal happiness if you promise to try out new perversions.

But that disgusting fellowship ruined it all! That stinking band of brothers encouraged him to confess his struggle and cut links with curvaceous Nancy! Yuck! My lustful demons couldn't even work during those Bible study meetings. The Maker himself was in their presence as soon as two or three of them convened and opened those blasted Bibles. His consistency with that fellowship and his humility to accept help, got him out of my cage. God's kindness then led him to horrid repentance. But we won't make that mistake with you. You are my fool. I always upgrade my strategy with you quiet ones. That's why this struggle will be older than your own kids. If I fancy, I may introduce one of them to it.

GRACE AND MERCY ARE POWERFUL TOOLS AGAINST ADDICTIONS.

On a happier note, I'm glad that you stopped dreaming about a happy marriage and godly offspring because that is never going to happen. Not on my watch. I will make sure of that. This struggle is customized to steal your passion, kill your dreams, and destroy your life. It's the job description our hellish high father has assigned us. Steal, kill, and destroy. I'm also glad that you've given up on the hope of a good relationship with your Maker. It's only logical. He is too boring, uptight, and full of rules.

Well, we'll show him who's in charge of this planet. It's too bad I couldn't get you to disbelieve in his existence. But at least I can get you to disbelieve in his power and goodness. The power of that bloody cross (oh, how we wish we could turn that day around) will never be available for you. I will make sure of that. You will never discover how much he loves you and forgives you. Grace and mercy are such dreadful tools against addictions.

But we often allow addicts to hear them as long as they are not balanced healthily with the message of the Maker's wrath. Without wrath, grace and mercy lose meaning and power, power to deliver fools like you. And if you do experience this power, I will be sure to convince you to trust in your effort and not his finished work on that Jewish hill.

Depend on those silly resolutions on your strength without his power. I'm glad your local church has adopted New Age teaching that avoids those Christian fundamental truths because they are offensive or not seeker-friendly enough. Stick in that church and you'll do just fine.

Anyway, I have to go now. You know, marriages to burn, youth to waste, regret to cause. My shift for the day is over but I will be back. I will wait for you to wake up tomorrow to repeat this beautiful cycle of slavery. But don't miss me too much when I'm away, fool. I'll invade your dreams with a few shameful, lustful fantasies and fearful visions. I can't sleep, you know. Hellish high father won't allow it, or I may find myself in the abyss. So, your night times must be restless with demonic torture for making me lose my rest.

Yours licentiously,

Lust

12

ACCOUNTABILITY

**EVERYONE SAYS THEY WANT COMMUNITY
AND FRIENDSHIP. BUT MENTION ACCOUNTABILITY
OR COMMITMENT TO PEOPLE, AND THEY
RUN THE OTHER WAY.
TIMOTHY KELLER**[25]

A young woman in her mid-twenties approached my wife and me about her fiancé. He had been emotionally and verbally abusive to her. He demanded sex every day and would throw a tantrum when she refused. She would give in to him out of fear. She was afraid to speak her mind and was not comfortable at all. When we asked her who kept her man accountable, she laughed. "Nobody tells Eric what to do.[26] He does what he wants and he knows what he knows." The girl wanted to end the relationship but was afraid of his reaction. She then admitted that the man serves in ministry at their church and is close to their pastor. We advised her to approach the pastor. She shook her head.

"Eric is a saint before his pastor. Everyone thinks he is waiting for sex until marriage, yet we fornicate every day. If his pastor found out he would be undone!"

We insisted that she must report to the pastor of the church. She was still adamant. The man had built such a pretentious image of himself to his authorities and his parents. He was hurting this woman. Nobody knew that he got drunk, abused drugs, and forced his way abusively onto his fiancée.

Another lady we met asked us whether she should accept to marry her boyfriend of two years. He wanted to propose to her. She could sense it coming. But she was worried that he kept his finances a secret. He refused to declare the source of his income and how much he makes. When she persisted, he blew his fuse and called her disrespectful and nosey. We advised the woman to approach a third party that keeps the man accountable. The woman said that the man detests accountability. When she suggested that they attend a seminar to help them clear the issue, he told her she may as well attend it since she is the one with the problem.

These are red flags. People who detest accountability will make horrible marriage partners. When you go through tough times, this will be a constant source of frustration. In our time ministering to couples, we notice that the men more often have an issue with accountability. Women generally warm up to the idea of accountability. Most are ready and willing to talk out their issues, although there are a few who aren't. Many men, on the other hand, operate as lone rangers.

One married man almost shed tears as he spoke of how his wife treated him. We knew the wife, so we called her to ask her to explain her side of the story. We got to see exactly what he was saying. She kept complaining incessantly that he was the problem in their marriage and she was unhappy. We asked her what percentage she contributed to the problem. She was shell-shocked. As far as she was concerned, she had no problems; he needed to change. We asked her if anyone kept her accountable. She went quiet again.

In that joint session, her husband spoke freely for the first time in their marriage. He mentioned several mean things she had done to him. We asked her if it was true. She shamefully accepted. We asked her if she thought her behaviour had any correlation to her husband's reactions. She struggled hearing the question. Nobody asked her such things. Nobody kept her accountable. She believed that her spouse changing was more urgent than her own changing to make the marriage better. She always saw herself as a victim because pride had entered her heart. She threw pity parties and was harsh and abrasive when provoked.

There are several reasons why we hear such horrible stories even from those in the church. Primarily, it is because the men and women are not truly walking with God and depending on his Word and Spirit. It could be that these men and women are not truly born again (see 2 Corinthians 13:5). Jesus warned us that at the end of time, church folk will get the scare of their lives to realize they are headed for the fires of hell and not the gates of God's Kingdom (see Matthew 7:21-23).

However, I want to focus on another reason that is often neglected. The reason that this bad behaviour persists among men and women is that these men have no intimate community of older, mature men who can rebuke and confront them when the need arises. In our interaction with several young married couples, we noticed that some men and women behave badly in their marriages because there is no one to challenge them when they are out of line.

For a number of them, their heavy involvement in ministry and their religious Sunday faces give the impression that they are good husbands and wives. Meanwhile, their spouses silently suffer uncivil, crude, and character-deficient behaviour in private. When these hurt spouses (mostly women) ask for help, we often ask them who keeps their partners accountable. They look at us with blank faces, unable to answer.

Marrying a man or woman who is not accountable to fellow men and women respectively is relational suicide. Why? Simply put, a man without accountability is a dangerous man. A woman without accountability is a dangerous woman. Often, lone rangers are custom-made prey for the enemy. Men and women who get into cycles of moral degeneration often have superficial friendships with fellow men and women. As I examine my heart, I notice that the more I stray from godliness, the more I hate accountability, and the more I reject it with pseudo-logical excuses. Conversely, the more I invite accountability in my life, the more I am empowered to live a godly life, and the more I accept it with humility.

A man without accountability is a dangerous man. A woman without accountability is a dangerous woman. One trademark of people who detest accountability is hypocrisy. They are two-faced. They have perfected the art of smiling, laughing, and looking the part. But they drop their masks when they get home and pick up the real faces. If you want to marry well, you must invite accountability into your life. Jesus spoke on the need for third-party accountability in our relationships.

> 'If your brother or sister sins, go and point out their fault, just between the two of you. If they listen to you, you have won them over. But if they will not listen, take one or two others along, so that "every matter may be established by the testimony of two or three witnesses." If they still refuse to listen, tell it to the church; and if they refuse to listen

> **MARRYING A MAN OR WOMAN WHO IS NOT ACCOUNTABLE TO FELLOW MEN AND WOMEN RESPECTIVELY IS RELATIONAL SUICIDE.**

even to the church, treat them as you would a pagan or a tax collector' (Matthew 18:15-17).

There are several other Scriptures that emphasize the need for accountable relationships. Accountability helps us become better through learning from others.

> As iron sharpens iron,
>> so one person sharpens another (Proverbs 27:17).

Accountability helps us remain humble in our spiritual walk as we help one another.

Brothers and sisters, if someone is caught in a sin, you who live by the Spirit should restore that person gently. But watch yourselves, or you also may be tempted. Carry each other's burdens, and in this way you will fulfil the law of Christ (Galatians 6:1-2).

Accountability offers a platform to receive healing through repentance and confession.

Therefore confess your sins to each other and pray for each other so that you may be healed. The prayer of a righteous person is powerful and effective (James 5:16).

Accountability is necessary for success in life.

> Two are better than one,
>> because they have a good return for their labour:
> if either of them falls down,
>> one can help the other up.
> But pity anyone who falls
>> and has no one to help them up.
> Also, if two lie down together, they will keep warm.

But how can one keep warm alone?
Though one may be overpowered,
   two can defend themselves.
A cord of three strands is not quickly broken
   (Ecclesiastes 4:9-12).

Accountability helps us remain on the narrow path of godliness.

> My brothers and sisters, if one of you should wander from
> the truth and someone should bring that person back,
> remember this: whoever turns a sinner from the error of
> their way will save them from death and cover a multitude
> of sins (James 5:19-20).

Men need to take this chapter seriously because God has a
special place in his heart for married women. Once you get
married, God actually says that he will not hear your prayers
if you are inconsiderate to her. The Bible says in 1 Peter 3:7,
"Husbands, in the same way be considerate as you live with
your wives, and treat them with respect as the weaker partner
and as heirs with you of the gracious gift of life, so that nothing
will hinder your prayers." One way to be a considerate
husband is to have men who will keep you accountable for
your behaviour. And you ought not wait until you are married;
you ought to start now so that you can marry well.

Men ought to have a band of brothers to keep them growing
and to keep them accountable. Women should have a
sisterhood for that very same purpose. So that things are not
inappropriate between the sexes, it is important that men and
women get accountability from their own genders. What
should this accountability look like?

THE CONTENT OF ACCOUNTABILITY

One of the key pillars that one should insist on in accountable relationships is confidentiality. Your accountability group must verbally agree to keep matters discussed in the group confidential. Proverbs 11:13 says, "A gossip betrays a confidence, but a trustworthy person keeps a secret." There are many people who have been hurt by a lack of confidentiality in their accountability groups.

Another pillar of accountable relationships is vulnerability. It makes no sense to belong to an accountability group and keep mum. There are men and women who relish hearing others speak of their issues but never disclose their own. It is dishonourable, cowardly, and immature to do so. If you cannot be vulnerable about your deepest weaknesses, you do not qualify to belong to an accountability group.

The third pillar of accountability is teachability. One of the most frustrating things about discipling people is that you teach them the truth, they say "amen", and then they do the very opposite. It is frustrating for a disciple-maker when his disciples are not teachable. It is equally frustrating when one who is kept accountable agrees with his or her head but does not follow through with his or her heart. Proverbs 12:15 says, "The way of fools seems right to them, but the wise listen to advice." If you belong to an accountability group, you must refuse to be a fool.

These three pillars are often lacking in accountable relationships because of pride. Proverbs 29:23 says, "Pride brings a person low, but the lowly in spirit gain honour." We

WE ARE CONCERNED ABOUT IMAGE AND NOT REALITY. THAT IS PRIDE.

want others to think we are doing well. We want to appear spiritual. We want to appear important and without weakness. We want to look like we know it all. We are concerned about image and not reality. That is pride. And pride makes you a fool. Listen to what Richard Baxter had to say about image:

> Study first to be whatever (judiciously) you desire to seem. Desire a thousand times more to be godly, than to seem so; and to be liberal, than to be thought so; and to be blameless from every secret or presumptuous sin, than to be esteemed such. And when you feel a desire to be accounted good, let it make you think how much more necessary and desirable it is to be good indeed. To be godly, is to be an heir of heaven: your salvation followeth it. But to be esteemed godly is of little profit to you.[27]

In order to marry well, you should be ready to embrace confidentiality, vulnerability, and teachability. It will do your future marriage good, and it will help you be a better spouse when the need for accountability rises.

THE STRUCTURE OF ACCOUNTABILITY

Once we are committed to being accountable, we need to flesh out the structure. Men and women should have accountability on three levels.

- Level one: older men and women whose marriages and lives you look up to.
- Level two: peers who go through the same life issues as you.
- Level three: younger men and women who look up to you.

We have many peer-accountability structures in the church. They are good, but they lack the authority to keep men and women from pretence. We need more level one and level three accountability structures.

Level One

Level one men and women are those you look up to. They ought to have thriving marriages. They ought to be spiritually sound and lead lives you admire. These are people who can speak into your life with authority. These are people to whom your partner is free to report you when you misbehave. Personally, I have a number of godly, male role models, whom my wife can run to and report any nonsensical behaviour that I insist on.

The primary roles of level one accountability partners are mentorship and teaching. The level one men and women should not be impressed by our accomplishments, personalities, and earthly successes. They should be well grounded in their identity and should not be intimidated by the money, influence, or charisma you have. These men and women should be fun enough to tease us but serious enough to point out that we have one life to live and cannot afford juvenile mistakes.

These men and women should have the capacity to encourage us when we are at our lows and be bold enough to deflate us when we are puffed up with pride. We should be free enough to laugh at a good joke with them, but never free enough to raise our voice at them. These men and women should be able to boldly and humbly confront weak pseudo-spiritual remarks like "don't judge me" or "keep out of my business" with the lion truth of God's Word without worrying about the fragility of our delicate little egos.

Level Two

Level two accountability involves men and women who are our peers in the walk of life. Many of them may be within your age group. Your best friends should come from this group of people and should be of the same sex. These men and women should be safe zones for you to talk about your deepest hurts, fears, and weaknesses. The primary roles of level two accountability partners are encouragement and spurring. They should be encouragers because they are going through the same life issues as you. They should spur you to be better by reminding you of the future you want.

Level Three

The final accountability system is level three. This involves those younger than you. These are those who look up to you. You play the role of a level one to them. They may be in high school or just fresh into college. These are people whom you should disciple and mentor. They should keep you on your toes because they emulate you.

The primary roles of level three accountability partners are to challenge you and to learn from you. We should have the confidence that Paul the apostle had with the Corinthians when leading the level three men and women. In 1 Corinthians 11:1 Paul says, "Follow my example, as I follow the example of Christ." That will challenge you to be Christlike. These young men and women should want a relationship just like yours. You should create time for them and pour your life into them.

If you do not invest in the younger generation, you will become bloated. If you invest in the younger generation, your own capacity to become better increases. This is what Jesus said in Matthew 13:12, "Whoever has will be given more, and they will have an abundance. Whoever does not have, even what they have will be taken from them."

When accountability is a part of your life, your capacity to marry well is healthy. When we are averse to accountability, we have probably hampered several chances at being good spouses, whether we realize it or not.

13

HURTS AND WOUNDS

**SEE TO IT THAT NO ONE FALLS SHORT OF THE GRACE OF GOD AND THAT NO BITTER ROOT GROWS UP TO CAUSE TROUBLE AND DEFILE MANY.
HEBREWS 12:15**

A young man wrote me a long email. He had dated his girl for four years and was planning to marry her. However, he was hesitant to do so. I asked him why. He said his girlfriend had slept with one of his friends and he had discovered the information by snooping on her phone. He felt guilty for not respecting her privacy; at the same time, he was compelled to confront her with his newfound information. He eventually did and confirmed the worst. He grew bitter and cynical about women.

A lady with whom I am friends on Facebook commented on an update of another mutual online friend. The mutual friend had written how she had come to the realization that there were some good men in this world. The lady angrily littered the comment section with expletives and phrases such as "all men are trash." The mutual friend confronted the verbal tirade calmly and pointed out that the woman might be harbouring bitterness from past hurts. It only made the woman angrier.

As we approach the end, we have to emphasize that marrying well can never take place without dealing with past hurts and wounds. For many young people, a number of past relationships are often characterized by regret and pain. I hope that as you have read the book this far, you have developed the humility to see areas where you messed up in your previous relationships. However, it's not only our exes that cause us hurt. It is possible that our own parents have hurt us as well. Relationships with our parents have an influence in our relationships with our significant others – especially relationships with our fathers.

It is said that a father is often a girl's first idea of what a husband should be. He is also a boy's first idea of what a man should be. Several sociologists will tell you that it has been proven that when fathers are absent, they negatively affect a child's well-being in a tremendous way. Chances of teenage pregnancies, poverty, and school dropouts are on the increase when fathers are missing. Absent fathers can leave their children with what psychologists call a father wound. A father wound is a painful emotional scar brought about by absent or difficult fathers.

Fathers can be present but still cause father wounds. They can be passive parents who fail to be involved in the lives of their children. They can fail to provide. They can fail to teach the truth. They can fail to tell their daughters that they are beautiful and leave them to fall prey to men who only use these words to take advantage of them. They can fail to call out the men in their sons and raise a generation of boys who don't know what masculinity entails. Present fathers can be abusive verbally, physically, and emotionally. They can scar their children and bring about father wounds.

The same can happen with mothers and their children. These parental influences affect how we choose life partners and how we respond to God's commands on marriage. There are ex-boyfriends and ex-girlfriends who remind us of painful memories with parents. Perhaps it is for that reason that they become exes. Even though one may have had great parental relationships, they can still harbour hurt from exes. The hurt could range from unexplained silence to infidelity. See what Scripture tells us:

> See to it that no one falls short of the grace of God and that no bitter root grows up to cause trouble and defile many (Hebrews 12:15).

BITTERNESS BLURS THE GRACE OF GOD

Hebrews 12:15 tells us that bitterness springs up when we fail to grasp God's grace. You cannot remain bitter at someone without thinking of yourself better than that person is. When you are bitter you often imagine, "How dare she do that!" or "How could he do that to me?" If you really analyze those thoughts, what we are really saying is, "I could never do what they did." Extrapolate this further and you realize that because you consider yourself above that person's actions, you eventually consider that person below you and yourself better than he or she is.

We remain bitter because we deem the offender's mistake to be so grand and unfathomable. If it were small, we'd graciously ignore and forget it. But since we deem the offence to be at a global level, we dwell on it and give it unblinking and undivided attention. The problem with that is that we focus on our offended hearts and our victimhood and we forget God's offended heart and our own sinful villainy.

When Jesus hung on the cross, he forgave the mistakes and abandoned bitterness when he said, "Father forgive (insert your name here), for they do not know what they are doing." Until you understand the gravity of your own sins and their grave offence to a holy God, you will have no incentive to let go of the bitterness you hold towards others. Jesus offered you forgiveness of your sins so that you would be saved.

I once had a friend who spread false rumours about me. He published the lies on Facebook. He texted a few of my close friends and told them that he had evidence that I was sleeping with each of their girlfriends. When the news came to me, I was livid! I remembered the command to pray for your enemies and so I decided to give it a go. The words could not leave my mouth. Each time I would begin to pray, I would stop halfway and just simmer in anger. Christ reminded me of his words, "Father forgive them for they do not know what they are doing." I argued with God's will. In my estimation, I should have prayed, "Father strike them down, for they know exactly what they are doing!"

UNTIL YOU UNDERSTAND THE GRAVITY OF YOUR OWN SINS AND THEIR GRAVE OFFENCE TO A HOLY GOD, YOU WILL HAVE NO INCENTIVE TO LET GO OF THE BITTERNESS YOU HOLD TOWARDS OTHERS.

But God allows us to see that we deserve to be on that cross and have no ground to hold bitterness in our hearts. If we are forgiven on the cross, we must then forgive any and every kind of offence towards us. When we forget how much God ought to be angry with us, but he loved us instead, we become bitter with those who have wronged us. I remained bitter at my friend for months because I shifted my focus from the cross and onto myself. When the Lord showed me that I had no right to vengeance because of his shed blood for me, I realized that the more hurt you are, the more glorious the cross will become to you.

The more bitter you are, the more wonderful you will realize grace is when you forgive. When the Lord was exhorting me to pray, he was actually delivering me from the root of bitterness. It was much later that I realized you cannot remain bitter at people you pray for. The more you pray for people, the more your heart lets go of the pain they have caused you. Prayer for your enemies is a powerful tool to appropriate the grace of God in your life when you feel hurt. Hurt and persecution is punishment to the world but a blessing in disguise to the believer.

ROOTS ARE HARDER TO DEAL WITH AS TIME GOES BY

Roots of a week-old tree have no power against the upward pull of my hand. But roots of a five-year-old tree are troublesome. They have entrenched themselves in the soil and have grown thick and strong. The older the tree, the harder it is to uproot it. The root of bitterness in our hearts must be uprooted quickly before it grows thick and strong. Let us look at the verse again. The Bible says that bitterness is a root, and roots are harder to deal with as time goes by. Hebrews 12:15 says, "See to it that no one falls short of the grace of God and that no bitter root grows up to cause trouble and defile many."

Uprooting a grown tree damages the land. An entrenched bitter root will damage our hearts if we delay dealing with it. I realized that the more I postponed dealing with the bitterness towards my friend, the harder it was to confront it. There were days it was even hard to sleep because I seethed in anger from this hurt. The world says time will heal. The Bible says time will cement the hurt in your heart if you don't forgive when the root is a seedling.

One reason I took too long to uproot my bitterness when I was offended by my friend is that I wanted him to earn my forgiveness. What I did not know is that forgiveness that has to be earned is not forgiveness at all. The bona fide signature of forgiveness is unmerited pardon. Forgiveness should not have to be earned by begging cries from the offender, appeasing gifts, or placating pleas to consider letting the hurt go. Why? Because forgiveness may be given freely but it is priceless. Forgiveness that has to be earned is a form of unforgiveness. It has its roots in the soil of pride and is enriched in the manure of hurt. The trick isn't necessarily to swallow one's pride but rather to vomit it out of your system altogether. To forgive is to give up the right to get even. Forgive without conditions, otherwise your hurt and pride will thicken and strengthen the root of bitterness.

DEALING WITH BITTERNESS THROUGH CONFESSION

As we read Hebrews 12:15 it also tells us, "see to it". Paul is addressing believers responding to the bitterness of fellow believers. I believe "seeing to it" means that we should be sensitive to people's hurts in the church. When you see a believer hurt, stop them, find out what's wrong, and pray with them. Even if they don't open up, offer prayer. This kind of encouragement will help kill the root of bitterness. If I deduce that if I am bitter, I need to confess it to fellow believers so that they encourage me; so that they see to it.

BITTERNESS AFFECTS RELATIONSHIPS

The verse says to see "that no bitter root grows up to cause trouble and defile many." I realized that I have one heart. And if it is bitter towards just one person, it cannot relate well with other people because it is the same heart. Hebrews 12:15 says bitterness causes trouble and defiles many. The fellowships and friendships around me will be poisoned. A person with unresolved bitterness will hurt others (cause trouble) and spread their bitterness like the flu because it is the only heart they have. The saying is true; hurt people hurt people. You have one heart. If that one heart is bitter towards just one person, it will affect your relationships with people who have no bearing on your bitterness. Even worse, that same heart cannot worship God if it's soaked in bitterness.

Our hearts cannot compartmentalize sin. One sin that is not dealt with affects the entire heart. I confessed my bitterness to my wife and to my Bible study members. If I had not, it could have ruined my marriage and the Bible study because of my pride. They prayed with me and encouraged me with their own past histories of bitterness. They reminded me that a focus on the cross eventually uproots the root of bitterness.

In my personal walk with Christ, I find that the ultimate antidote to any sin, and in our case bitterness, is to get closer to God. The closer you get to God, the more sinful you realize you are, thus, the more forgiven you realize you are. And the more forgiven you realize you are, the more moved you become by the sacrifice on the cross. Getting closer to God is like a black spot approaching the filament of a bright white bulb. The closer it gets to the white light of the filament, the darker it seems. Even a semi-white spot looks stained in contrast to pure white. The closer you get to God, the more you realize how dark your heart really is and how badly you need his grace. No good works, gifts to charity, or

> **FORGIVENESS IS GIVING UP THE RIGHT TO GET EVEN AND LEAVING THE SITUATION IN GOD'S HANDS.**

prayer can wash away that darkness and make you white before the filament. Getting close to God cannot make you feel better about yourself; if anything, it makes you humble in the light of his holiness and majesty.

Bitterness does the opposite; it trumps others and elevates self. If I feel morally superior, spiritually greater, theologically sounder than those around me, I only reveal that my dark heart has moved away from the white filament; I have become proud and I need to go back to the light to be humbled. A proud heart insists on maintaining its bitterness. Jesus said in Matthew 6:15, "But if you do not forgive others their sins, your Father will not forgive your sins." A bitter, proud heart may point out a Pharisee, forgetting that they may be a bigger Pharisee. Jesus himself was not a Pharisee about Pharisees; he was not intolerant towards intolerant people.

In this lifetime, if we confess our need for the Saviour, Christ Jesus, and the need to be saved from the blackness of our sinful, bitter hearts, he gives us a white coat of righteousness to cover our black hearts and take away our bitterness. And on that day when we shall see him return, our black hearts shall be thoroughly sanctified to match the white filament, not by our efforts, not by our morals, not by our good deeds but by his grace and mercy alone.

Some people think that if they forgive their partner, they will be letting them go scot free. Forgiveness does not mean you are endorsing this person's bad behaviour. Forgiveness is giving up the right to get even and leaving the situation in God's hands. Hear what the Word of God says in Romans 12:19-21:

> Do not take revenge, my dear friends, but leave room for God's wrath, for it is written: 'It is mine to avenge; I will repay,' says the Lord. On the contrary:

'If your enemy is hungry, feed him;
     if he is thirsty, give him something to drink.
  In doing this, you will heap burning coals on
       his head.'

Do not be overcome by evil, but overcome evil with good.

Ultimately, unforgiveness makes you a potentially horrible spouse. The constant pattern of a marriage is overlooking offences and forgiving your spouse. If you don't train yourself to forgive, you will train yourself to fail at your marriage. You must realize that even after you forgive, the pain may still come. I like to think of forgiveness like a stubborn stain. At times you rub and rub but the stain still remains. However, with time and patience and consistent rubbing, the stain disappears. We must forgive as often as we recall the pain. We must forgive as often as we feel the hurt. Jesus said to forgive 70 times seven.

When you refuse to forgive someone, you are really saying to that person, "What you did was so bad, I could never do that." The deeper thing we are really saying is "I am better than you." An unforgiving heart can never escape the reality of being a proud heart. The solution to this kind of pride, and consequently the solution to forgiving, is to bask in the forgiveness of the gospel. You must imbibe deeply the fact that Christ (God incarnate) was crucified in your place. But it will only work if:

- You understand the gravity of your own sin towards God.

- You measure that gravity against his holiness and comprehend that his forgiveness for you is indeed amazing grace.

- You watch your pride melt and your confidence in being forgiven grow.
- You appropriate that grace to those who have hurt you.
- You open the prison door of forgiveness only to discover that you were the prisoner.

Some relationships are not salvaged after a hurtful experience. But we must remember that the Bible calls us to do everything possible to reconcile. Romans 12:18 says, "If it is possible, as far as it depends on you, live at peace with everyone." The Bible admits that the possibility may lack, but we must ensure we have done everything possible on our part. With a marriage, we are compelled to do so because God hates divorce (Malachi 2:16). For that reconciliation to take place it requires people to take stock of the relationship. What was lost? How much of it was lost? What was gained? Was it a good gain or a bad gain? You then enter into intentional habits that help you recover the good that was lost, maintain the good that was gained, and lose the bad that was earned as a result of the hurt. These habits are confined to the three levels of friendship we tackled earlier in the book:[28]

- Supernatural habits: formative spiritual habits such as corporate prayer and studying the Word help reconciliation.
- Natural habits: joint relaxing leisure activities that are dear to both of you help reconciliation take place, e.g., a walk, a movie, a game night, etc.
- Romantic habits: rekindling the love with a romantic friend by starting the relationship afresh. Engage deeply in your partner's love languages and meet her or his gender-specific needs we mentioned in chapter six.

As you do this, you must choose to risk, to trust again by faith. In the process, there may be emotional upheavals, but you must address them as the psalmists  did. The book of Psalms is arguably the most emotional book in the Bible. In it are joys, cries, pains, and exultations. All 150 chapters of the Psalms are warranted by God for one reason; they don't Facebook their emotions; they face God. King David vehemently cries out to God concerning his enemies in several chapters in the Psalms. He is angry! He doesn't vent it out in the public square. Neither does he simmer about it in silence. He prays his feelings.

When the wicked are succeeding in Psalm 73, Asaph does not write angry tweets of how unfair life is. At the same time, he doesn't ignore what he feels and say it is none of his business. No, he prays his emotions. He takes the situation to God. Every overwhelming emotion a believer has should be channelled to God. Remember, I said channelled *to* God and not channelled *at* God. When you angrily blame God for the death of a loved one, that is channelling *at* God and it is not only improper but myopic as well. When we pray our emotions, we go through a cycle of adoring, confessing, thanking, and interceding because of how we feel, and it heals us. It takes the burden from our hearts into the able arms of God.

How do we adore, confess, thank, and intercede using our emotions? When you see the beauty of creation and it takes your breath away, you use your awed emotion to adore the Creator of planet Earth and it pleases him. When you feel guilty for something wrong you've done, you go before God and confess your mistake, ask him to give you a clean heart, he does, and it pleases him. When you score an A in your test, you channel that joy by thanking God for your opportunities and resources at school, he perceives your gratefulness, and it pleases him. When you see injustice in society that makes you angry, you channel that anger to God, you pray for divine intervention in that area of injustice, and it pleases him. How does it please him? It pleases him because God responds to your prayer and that of many believers and heals the injustice through his powerful ways.

YOUR PRAYER HEALS THE HURTING

What happens when we don't channel our emotions to God? You see that sunset another time and you get used to it. You become indifferent and unaware of his majesty and beautiful creation even after seeing it many times. That's how vices such as environmental degradation take over. Forests are cut to make money because the populace did not channel their awe of its beauty to God. They got used to it and didn't see a problem when it was destroyed.

When you feel that guilt and fail to channel it to God, you become self-absorbed, develop self-pity, and begin to think thoughts like: "Everyone is against me." "I'm no good." "God hates me." You become conscious of every mistake you make because the guilt eats at you and you become hostile, always saying stuff like, "Don't judge me!" God will judge you in the end and the root cause is channelling your emotions anywhere but towards God.

When you score that A grade and fail to channel your emotional joy to God through thanksgiving, you become proud and think highly of yourself because of what you accomplished. All it takes is scoring a C or a B and your tower of A's falls to the ground. But when your joy is channelled to God through thanksgiving, you remember that you are but dust and that

God is the big guy behind all your achievements. Even if you score a D, you are comfortable because you know you rest within the parameters of God's power despite the test outcome.

When you see injustice and angrily write a status update about it or tweet it, you not only do nothing to change it, but you deny the people the power of God to intervene spiritually. Emotion not channelled to God is wasted emotion; pray your emotions.

And when we pray our emotions, we allow ourselves to function as God desires. We cry, we laugh, we write what we feel, and we become vulnerable. Praying our emotions brings healing and satisfaction unlike venting and simmering.

The book of Psalms has several instances where writers like King David are fed up and angry, pleased and excited, guilty and overcome. Many believers think that to be a Christian means not to express yourself at all so that you can be seen as a saint. God differs. Others believe that it means shouting **PRAYING OUR EMOTIONS BRINGS HEALING AND SATISFACTION.** at rooftops against evils. Nay! Pray your emotions. The next time you see hungry children dying, lend a helping hand through donation. If you are not able to help actively, don't just tweet an empathetic update, pray about it. Every human being constantly deals with emotions. There is hardly a minute that passes by when an emotion is not active in you. If our emotions are working 24/7, then it means we need to pray them 24/7. In doing so we may just fulfil God's command in 1 Thessalonians 5:17, "Pray continually."

God calls us as Christians, true followers of Jesus, to follow him without fear, without holding on to bitterness and unforgiveness, without pride and self-pity, without so many other vices that develop from corrupted emotions. Whenever they raise their ugly heads, don't vent them, don't simmer them, pray them.

WHEN YOU ARE HURT BY YOUR PARTNER

Pastor John Wesley Nguuh preached in our wedding from Colossians 1 and 2 and he did a great job at giving us last-minute pieces of advice before we became man and wife. One common theme in all those sermons I have heard is this: your spouse will hurt you. When I heard it, at first I was perplexed. What a way to ruin a magical moment! Why would I want to hear, minutes before getting married, that my wife will hurt me? Well, it's necessary because that is the naked truth that the world won't tell you. After the magic of the day is spent, you are married to a human being. For the follower of Jesus, this is an especially important thing to consider because often we think that since our spouse's sins are forgiven, their capacity to sin is also erased. Not so!

When I say your spouse will hurt you, there are self-preserving people who may say, "Aha, that's why you should sign a prenup!" Well, for starters, if you are going to sign a prenup, then you are not mature enough to get married in the first place. Secondly, a prenup may protect your favourite sofa but it can't stop a breaking heart. Saying your partner will hurt you is not saying, "Watch out! He or she is going cheat on you anytime now!" What we are saying is that hurt is often unpredictable. Unlike the major deal breakers for many people such as infidelity and violence, most hurts in marriage will range between our wounded pride and our fear when certain buttons are pressed. The Scriptures in 1 Peter 2:21-24 give us an example to follow:

> To this you were called, because Christ suffered for you, leaving you an example, that you should follow in his steps.

> 'He committed no sin,
>> and no deceit was found in his mouth.'

When they hurled their insults at him, he did not retaliate; when he suffered, he made no threats. Instead, he entrusted himself to him who judges justly. 'He himself bore our sins' in his body on the cross, so that we might die to sins and live for righteousness; 'by his wounds you have been healed.'

Jesus Christ is often hurt by his spouse, the church. Yet Christ sets an example for us to follow when he is hurt by the world he created. Christ redeems his spouse, and we ought to do so too. Let us dissect 1 Peter 2:21-24 a bit.

1. Know That You Will Suffer

> To this you were called, because Christ suffered for you, leaving you an example, that you should follow in his steps (1 Peter 2:21).

One of the top lies that people believe about the Christian faith is that if I become a Christian, God won't allow anything bad to happen to me. The second lie they believe is that if I become a good Christian and stick to the rules, God will be my personal bodyguard and hurt those who hurt me. The truth is that God will allow suffering to build your character. He has done that since he started saving the world in Genesis and we are no exception. God is more interested in who you become than in how you feel in a brief moment of pain. Why? Because the joy of maturity after the pain outweighs the brief moments of pain.

Jesus Christ did not suffer so that the Christian will never suffer but, more importantly, so that *when* the Christian does suffer, he or she will overcome. He not only picked up the cross for us; he also showed us how to pick up ours. Christ is not only the hero that saves us from pain; he is also the exemplar of how to handle the pain that is sure to come. And when our relationships cause us to hurt, we ought to remember that sin is the ultimate cause of suffering and that sin is temporal.

Fyodor Dostoyevsky, in his classic novel *The Brothers Karamazov*, paints a truth about all pain and suffering through a character named Ivan. Ivan is an atheist and struggles to accept the world of his brother who serves as a monk. He has lunch with his brother, Alexei, and eventually admits that even he understands that all suffering will be made up for in the end. He states:

> I believe like a child that suffering will be healed and made up for, that all the humiliating absurdity of human contradictions will vanish like a pitiful mirage, like the despicable fabrication of the impotent and infinitely small Euclidian mind of man.[29]

Don't allow temporal suffering to deny you an eternal blessing. God will reward each person according to his or her work. Is your behaviour in response to suffering in your relationship producing an eternal, imperishable reward kept in heaven for you, or it is storing up results that will be consumed by fire despite your salvation?

2. Watch Your Mouth

> "He committed no sin, and no deceit was found in his mouth" (1 Peter 2:22).

No other time are our mouths more dangerous than when we suffer. In the height of human suffering, Christ Jesus kept his mouth shut. Matthew 12:36 says that on the day of judgement everyone will account for every careless word they spoke on Earth. Proverbs 18:21 says death and life are in the power of the tongue "and those who love it will eat its fruit". Unprocessed words will only cause more hurt. Hurt people end up hurting people. I have personally found it necessary to retreat in prayer when I am hurt and angry. When the Lord has processed my thoughts and words, I start to see my share of the problem that I was previously blind to. And even when I don't see the solution after prayer, the Lord has often prompted me to extend grace to those that hurt me, just as he did for me on that cross.

One evening when hanging out with a group of people, one of us shouted at a certain attendant of the place we were visiting because the service was horrible. I confronted the friend and asked if he liked being shouted at. His answer was no. Some friends came to his defence stating that the attendant deserved the shouting because she had not served us well. I was relieved when most of the people at the table disagreed. One friend said, "I don't like being shouted at; I don't think others like it when I do it." One opponent argued that we are suffering from the horrible service and we deserved to express how we felt. When she was countered by another who asked, "But is that how a Christian ought to act?" the unfortunate response came, "We are Christians, but you have to be tough at times."

And on that premise, I saw the root of my friends' attitudes and actions as far as their mouths were **OUR SPEECH REVEALS THE STATE OF OUR HEARTS.** concerned. Often those who state, "We are Christians but . . . " have no desire to live out the Christian life. Christ was guiltless but no guile was found on his lips. And Christ himself was cognisant of the suffering we would endure, but he never required us to be tough and mean. He said in Matthew 10:16 that we ought to be innocent as doves but shrewd as snakes. What does that mean? That means that you can emerge victorious even after you suffer if you apply biblical wisdom such as Ephesians 4:26a: "In your anger do not sin." Ephesians 4:29 says, "Do not let any unwholesome talk come out of your mouths, but only what is helpful for building others up according to their needs, that it may benefit those who listen."

When we suffer, do our mouths build up those we speak to or does it tear them down and embarrass them? When we suffer, can those who hear our conversations receive a dose of grace? Can they see us like Christ? Ultimately, our speech reveals the state of our hearts. See what James 3:6-12 says:

> The tongue also is a fire, a world of evil among the parts of the body. It corrupts the whole body, sets the whole course of one's life on fire, and is itself set on fire by hell.

> All kinds of animals, birds, reptiles and sea creatures are being tamed and have been tamed by mankind, but no human being can tame the tongue. It is a restless evil, full of deadly poison.

> With the tongue we praise our Lord and Father, and with it we curse human beings who have been made in God's likeness. Out of the same mouth come praise and cursing. My brothers and sisters, this should not be. Can both fresh water and salt water flow from the same spring? My brothers and sisters, can a fig-tree bear olives, or a grapevine bear figs? Neither can a salt spring produce fresh water.

When we suffer, our love is also tested. Many people claim to love God but treat fellow human beings like trash. John charges us to consider our ways in 1 John 4:20, "Whoever claims to love God yet hates a brother or sister is a liar. For whoever does not love their brother or sister, whom they have seen, cannot love God whom they have not seen."

3. Give up the Right to Retaliate

When they hurled their insults at him, he did not retaliate (1 Peter 2:23a).

Christ set the bar. You cannot sin if you have been sinned against. That is the bar he has set. Often, people retaliate intentionally for an offence that their partner made accidentally. Revenge is an ultimate mark of a lack of Christlikeness. At the heart of Christianity is a perfect God who forgave sinful people. At the heart of revenge is an attitude that counters God's work on the cross. I like that Jesus tells us that if we don't forgive those who have hurt us, neither will God forgive us. It is plain and simple. Matthew 6:15 says, "But if you do not forgive others their sins, your Father will not forgive your sins."

What do you do? Look at what 1 Peter 2:23c says, that he "entrusted himself to him who judges justly". Christ left vengeance to God, who judges justly. You ought to do the same. Many people have misconceptions about forgiveness. Some think that if they forgive their spouse, they are endorsing the sin against them. Remember that forgiveness is to take the keys and open the prison gates only to discover that the prisoner was you. That is why lack of forgiveness does not ultimately and eternally hurt the offender but rather the offended.

4. Do Not Threaten or Punish

When he suffered, he made no threats (1 Peter 2:23b).

A couple who was planning to get married came to speak to me. They had a tough time because each time they had a disagreement, the women threatened to call off the engagement. This behaviour will replicate itself in marriage. One way spouses can do this is to deny each other conjugal rights. Denying conjugal rights is not only dangerous to your sexual life but also sinful in the eyes of God. The Lord says in 1 Corinthians 7:4-5:

> The wife does not have authority over her own body but yields it to her husband. In the same way, the husband does not have authority over his own body but yields it to his wife. Do not deprive each other except perhaps by mutual consent and for a time, so that you may devote yourselves to prayer. Then come together again so that Satan will not tempt you because of your lack of self-control.

Of course, there are countless other ways spouses can threaten and punish each other when they are hurt. For example, the self-preserving spouse once hurt fears being hurt again. Often this spouse tends to believe that their marriage is meant to be magical and devoid of any strife. When disagreement occurs, the spouse acts as if something strange were happening to him or her. To cordon their space from further hurt, these spouses punish their partner through indifference or ignoring them.

Indifference and ignoring your spouse may look like a wise tactic, but it is otherwise; it is lazy and ineffective. The logic behind such a spouse's tactic is, "I won't be close to her or him, so that when my spouse hurts me, it won't sting so bad." Don't treat a marriage like a war zone. The hurts will only get worse.

Hurt will come. Someone may be afraid of trusting and loving again because the risk of being hurt is too high. Perhaps you have been taken advantage of in the past. The solution is to still look to Christ. He risked everything to love you and be in a relationship with you, yet you still hurt him. He gave everything knowing you would still hurt him. And only that leap of faith guarantees you a future after death. We often need to take that leap of faith. We cannot know everything. Life is lived forwards but only understood by looking backwards.

Finally, you can avoid unnecessary hurt by being intentional in your relationship. Boundaries with the opposite sex won't be kept naturally. Purity won't be observed naturally. Faithfulness won't be established naturally. Exclusivity won't be maintained naturally. Friendship won't grow naturally. Good communication won't occur naturally. Romance won't bud naturally.

All these pillars that support a great man-woman union must be done intentionally, purposefully, and diligently, if you want a thriving relationship. If you think that these things will be natural once you start dating, you will hurt your partner. And you will be surprised to learn that anything but an intentional commitment to things that matter is an unintentional commitment to things that do not matter. If you are not intentionally committed to making your marriage work, you are unintentionally committed to making it fail.

14

HAPPILY EVER AFTER

FOR GOD SO LOVED THE WORLD THAT HE GAVE HIS ONE AND ONLY SON, THAT WHOEVER BELIEVES IN HIM SHALL NOT PERISH BUT HAVE ETERNAL LIFE. FOR GOD DID NOT SEND HIS SON INTO THE WORLD TO CONDEMN THE WORLD, BUT TO SAVE THE WORLD THROUGH HIM.
JOHN 3:16-17

The man and the woman had been walking for nearly three hours. The woman lagged behind. Her feet were sore and her calves were burning with every step she took. Still, she kept going because he wouldn't stop. The man looked strong enough to keep walking for two days. His muscles tightened with every step across the rugged terrain.

The ground in this part of the land was different. It was not as beautiful as where they came from. It seemed to rebel against the beautiful environment. It was full of briars, thorns and thistles. A few metres ahead was the forest, west of the Euphrates river. None of them had ventured this far before. When the man finally stopped for the first time, the woman dropped to the ground relieved. She needed a rest. He angled his head slightly to catch a glimpse of her from the corner of his eye. He despised her. He wanted nothing to do with her. The sight of her was putrefying.

He noticed she was looking back at him. Past the long ebony hair that partly shrouded her face were equally sinister eyes. She loathed him. She was burning with rage towards him. Could he not see that she was tired? Could he not realize that her body could no longer take a step further? Was he always this inconsiderate? As soon as they settled, she would have a plan. Leave the man. Get as far away from him as possible.

"Get up," the man said. The ice in his tone was evident. The look on his face said that he knew it was. "It's almost dusk, we need to find a shalom."

She stared at him, incredulous. Was he serious?

"I'm not going anywhere," she replied matching his nasty inflection. "You should have thought about that before losing our home."

He let her poisonous words sink like a dagger. He said nothing. His thoughts murdered her. She was not worth replying.

"I can't believe you told him I was responsible," she continued. She shook her head in disbelief and then she spat on the ground. She wished that the ground was his face so that he could feel her frustration. She wanted him to know the pain she felt. The man said nothing. He just stood there in silence.

"And I can't believe that we lost everything we had. Could you not pack more?" The man looked at the sack in his hand. Apart from a few choice fruits, it held nothing else but lots and lots of air. She saw him search for a response but knew she had him pinned.

"Plus, we can't find a shalom, you lost the only one we had," the woman added, not shifting her attacking stance. Then suddenly, like an overdue volcano, the man erupted. He tossed the sack on the ground and marched towards her with bloodshot eyes and clenched fists.

"You blame me, woman! You dare blame me!"

The woman did not expect his flare-up, but she figured she needed to remain in control to hurt him more.

"Yes," she replied placidly, "I blame you, Adam. You were meant to protect me, but you failed. That's all you are, a failure of humanity."

"Protect you! Protect you from what? From the witchcraft of that blasted serpent that you colluded with? You believed him!" He pointed a warning finger at her, "Don't you dare make this my fault. You tricked me into his sorcery with your harlotry. Who knows what spell you placed over me?"

The woman laughed. She grabbed her belly and let out a deep, sinister, provocative laugh. It was so loud and full of spite, that Adam could almost feel it contort his face. She rose to her feet despite their aching and laughed some more.

"Stop it!" he commanded, but it only encouraged her. He knew why she laughed. There was something wrong with him. He had started denying claims of basic facts and was lying even about what he knew to be true. He knew he was under no spell when she offered him the accursed fruit he was warned not to eat. He knew she was deceived. He knew his lack of moral tenacity made the situation worse. He knew they lost Eden because he listened to her. He knew it but he would not accept it.

He was conflicted within himself. The thing he wanted to do, he did not, and that which he did not want to do, he found himself doing. And so it was, that the man did not want to strike his wife, but he did. His hand flew across her soft cheek and made a sharp clap that echoed in the trees above them.

The woman staggered in horror as her frail frame lost balance and fell in a thicket of briars. As she crashed to the ground squealing in pain, he covered his hand over his mouth. His eyes widened at the realization of his actions.

"Oh, my goodness, what have I done! I'm sorry!"

Adam, realizing his folly, placed his hands on his head in regret. His actions surprised him. He reached out to pull her from the thorny bush, but she wouldn't let him. Her arms and legs were striped with red. She was bleeding. She pulled her hands against the briars that punctured her delicate skin. She was still absorbing the fact that he struck her.

Surely, it wasn't him. It must have been a falling tree branch or something. But when she saw him hovering over her extending a hand of help and apologising profusely for his misdeed, the fact was confirmed. She resisted Adam's attempt to assist her. A boiling rage within her wanted to strike back. She clenched her bleeding fists, but a few briars stuck on her palm forced her to open them in pain. He reached for her palms and pulled out a few briars. When she regained composure, she opened her mouth to say the vilest things

THE THING HE WANTED TO DO, HE DID NOT, AND THAT WHICH HE DID NOT WANT TO DO, HE FOUND HIMSELF DOING.

her mind had ever imagined. But her mouth did not cooperate with her thoughts. Instead of abuse, came out a whimper. She fell to her knees and began to sob loudly. Adam was riddled with guilt. He fell to his knees to comfort her. Noticing her husband's attempt to make peace, she shoved him with all the energy her body could muster. She then picked herself up and ran past him into the dark forest ahead.

"Look, wait! I'm sorry!" He wanted to run after her, but his legs wouldn't allow him. No, not his legs. His mind and his heart. His pride wouldn't allow him. He watched his wife in her sheepskin tunic run into unknown parts of the land, without looking back, drying tears from her eyes.

Fine, let her go! She deserves to be disciplined anyway!

Three hours passed and his wife had not returned. The sun began to set, and Adam decided to pitch camp for the evening. The night wind was brutal. It was unusually cold and the shadows in the twilight seemed exceptionally dark. He lit a fire to keep himself warm and to scatter the scary shadows. The man sighed heavily as he pulled a few fruits from the sack to feast on. He barely ate one. His mind troubled him. He was concerned for his wife. He bowed to the pressure of self-pity and began to blame himself amidst sobs and curses. He desired death. What had he done? And before he contemplated it a second further, he felt a warm hand behind his shoulder. He felt brief ecstatic joy at the thought of his wife having returned. He whirled in anticipation and came face to face with someone else – a man in a radiant white tunic.

"Elohim!"

"Adam."

"Lord, I am so sorry," Adam said falling prostrate.

"What is done is done. It shall be atoned for, beloved. Go; find your wife. She's in grave danger."

"What?" he asked. Adam tried processing what the Lord said. Atonement. Could his error be reversed? Could they return home? But then something else stole his mind's attention. The last part of his sentence about his wife being in danger. He dried his tears and jumped to his sturdy feet.

"What kind of danger?"

"Leopards."

"The leopards are friendly; they always have been."

"The curse has changed them, beloved. They will maul her, and she will die, Adam. Arise and protect her."

Then he was gone. Adam looked around. He was alone. But he knew that the love of his life was in trouble. He could feel it like a deep pit in the stomach. They were one. Her pain was his pain. Adam picked up a stick of fire from the flames and ventured into the dark forest to rescue his bride from the darkness.

HAPPILY EVER AFTER

The story above is simply my own imagination and should not be used for theological teaching; it should simply be taken at face value as fiction. That is how I imagine life for Adam and Eve proceeded after the Fall. The beautiful story at the beginning was marred by sin. Intimacy was crushed and pride took over. It's the same for us. The capacity to marry well is hindered by our sin. Imagine a world where Adam and Eve never sinned. Imagine a world without crime. Or perhaps imagine a world where Adam and Eve did sin but not in chapter three. Imagine the fall of man happening in Genesis 17. That means we would have 16 solid chapters of what a good marriage looks like. We would have 16 solid chapters of what the world should be like. We wouldn't need to write relationship books; we'd just need to do quiet time in the first 16 chapters of Genesis. Wouldn't that be something? I want to adopt a middle ground between the two alternatives. I heard the following explanation from Pastor Robert Morris of Gateway Church.

Suppose Adam was given some fruit by Eve after she had eaten some and he declined. Suppose Adam refused to partake in the deception of Eve and stood by the command of God. Then God would come down in the cool of the day to talk to Adam, and Eve would possibly run and hide for fear and shame.

"Adam, we need to talk."

Adam glances behind to see his sinful wife hiding behind a bush trying to get cover for her nakedness.

"Um . . . yeah! Sure thing, Lord."

They begin the walk in silence. God finally breaks it.

"Adam, your wife has sinned."

"I know, Lord." He sighs.

"Well, Adam," the Lord says, "she has to die."

"Die?" Adam asks bewildered! "But why?"

"Well, Adam. The wages of sin is death. She sinned and she has to die."

"But I love her," Adam says softly.

"Well, I could make you another one," God offers. They keep walking in silence. Adam is pensive.

"But I don't want another one; I want her," Adam responds.

"Well, someone has to die," God states unequivocally.

Adam remains quiet for a while. They keep walking in silence. Then he stops. He sighs and turns to the Lord.

"Take me instead, Lord," Adam offers. "I will lay down my life for my bride."

And in an act of selfless love, Adam would be slain for the sin of Eve. And he would have bled and died to atone for her sin. But since Adam was sinless, he wouldn't have been kept  down by death. Death would have coughed him up and life would have hold of him again. Adam would come back from the grave a new man. Eve would be forgiven, her sin dealt with, and they would live happily ever after.

What an incredible story, right? It sounds like a beautiful fantasy. But Pastor Robert Morris proceeded to say that it's not. You see, more than 2000 years ago, the Bible tells us that there was another man like Adam. The Bible calls him the last Adam – Jesus Christ. And Morris likes to imagine that God must have had a similar conversation with the last Adam. It's not a perfect conversation because we know Christ is God, but it sends the point home if you allow it some flexibility.

"Jesus, we need to talk."

They begin the walk in silence. God the Father finally breaks it.

"Jesus, your bride has sinned."

"I know, Lord." He sighs.

"Well, Jesus," the Lord says, "She has to die."

"Die? But why?"

"Well, Jesus. The wages of sin are death. She sinned and she has to die."

"But I love her," Jesus says.

"Well, I could make you another one," God offers. They keep walking in silence.

"But I don't want another one; I want her," Jesus responds.

"Well, Son, someone has to die," God the Father states unequivocally.

Jesus sighs and turns to the Lord.

"Take me instead; I will lay down my life for my bride."

And in the greatest act of love, the last Adam laid down his life for his sinful bride who deserved death. And since he was a sinless man, death could not hold him down. He arose to new life, a new man, and his bride's sin was atoned for.

For God so loved the world that he gave his one and only Son, that whoever believes in him shall not perish but have eternal life. For God did not send his Son into the world to condemn the world, but to save the world through him (John 3:16-17).

Because Jesus intervened, we have a happily-ever-after in our eternity. Our relationships can taste that glimpse of eternity when we have him in our midst. If we have the last Adam as our priority, everything else will fall into place, even if we don't get married. We will realize that our greatest reward is not hearing the words, "I do", but rather hearing, "Well done, good and faithful servant." The seal to marrying well is to end

OUR RELATIONSHIPS CAN TASTE THAT GLIMPSE OF ETERNITY WHEN WE HAVE HIM IN OUR MIDST.

where we started – God first. We must be in him in order to remain sober in a world where relationships are going crazy. He proposed to us on that cross when he bled and died. If we accept his proposal, we will have the joy and the marriage we have always longed for.

This is the end of the book. I hope it has been of significant value to you. I pray that you will practise all that you learned in accordance with Jesus's words in John 13:17. I also pray that you will be spiritually alert. It's a spiritual war we are facing when we see marriages crumble. May yours be different through the power of the Holy Spirit. May your future generations be blessed because you obeyed. You may not be able to change your ancestors, but you can influence your descendants.

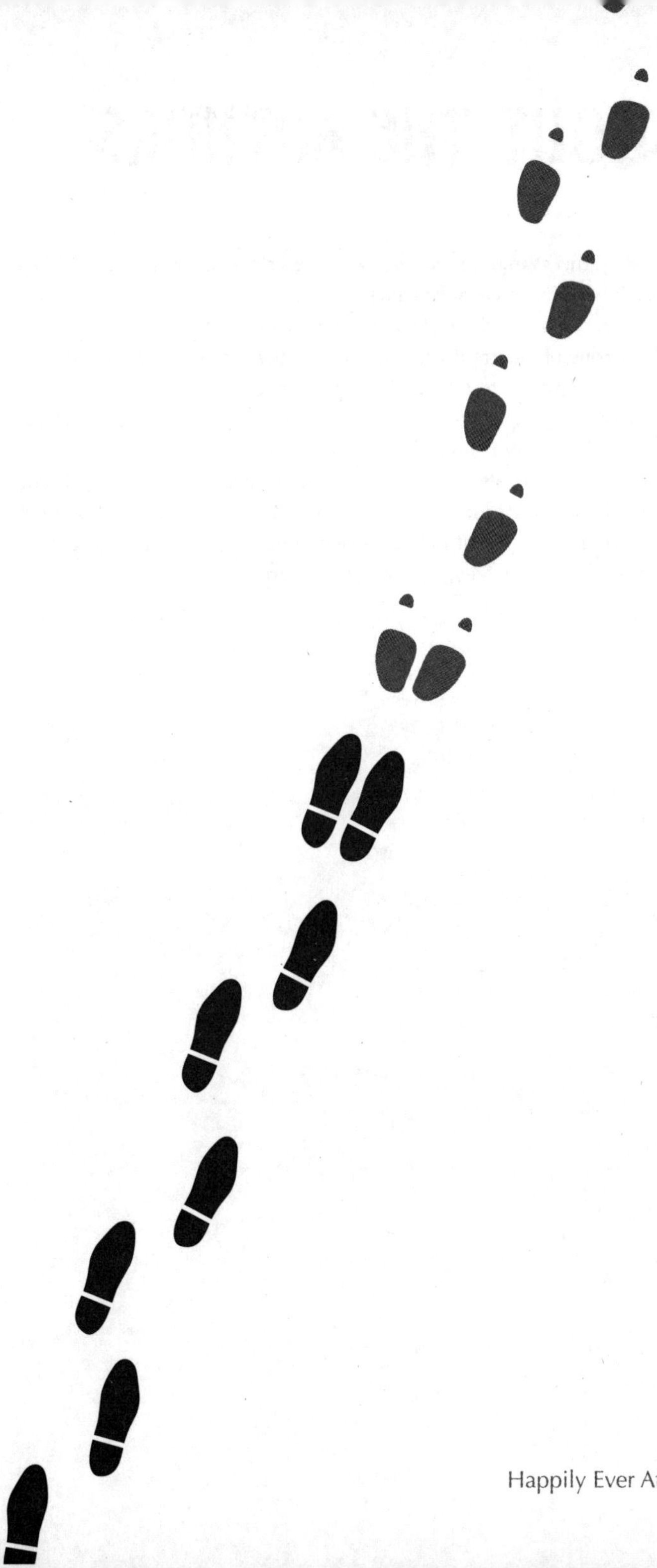

ABOUT THE AUTHORS

Ernest and Waturi Wamboye have been married since September 2012. They have two daughters: Thandiwe and Ivanna. The Wamboyes are passionate to see the gospel of Jesus Christ clearly taught and understood in our post-modern world. They are champions of biblical discipleship and furthering the Kingdom of God by transforming one person at a time. They are the founders of The Relationship Centre Ltd (TRC), an organization that aims to promote biblical family values in contemporary urban communities. Under the umbrella of TRC they run the following ministries: *Boy Meets Girl*, a quarterly relationships forum to help young people marry well, *Powerhouse*, a men's pornography addiction recovery program, and *Dating Clinic*, a couples' premarital and post-marital forum. Ernest is also the author of three other books. You can keep up with their award-winning blog, Pen Strokes: www.penstrokes.co.ke.

ENDNOTES

1   Jimmy Evans, "Are Millennials Afraid of Marriage?" *Bible Gateway* (blog), April 30, 2020, https://www.biblegateway.com/blog/2020/04/are-millennials-afraid-of-marriage/.

2   C. S. Lewis, *Mere Christianity* (New York: MacMillan, 1952), 31.

3   Timothy Keller, *Walking with God Through Pain and Suffering* (New York: Riverhead Books, 2013), 123.

4   Bruce Marshall, *The World, The Flesh, and Father Smith* (Scotland: Houghton Mifflin, 1945), 108.

5   Timothy Keller with Kathy Keller, *The Meaning of Marriage: Facing the Complexities of Commitment with the Wisdom of God* (New York: Penguin Random House Company, 2011), 231.

6   Timothy Keller (@timkellernyc), "You are under qualified for the job of master and commander of your own life.", Twitter, June 11, 2018, https://twitter.com/timkellernyc/status/1006236882282450944.

7   Ken Graves, *Master, Mission, Mate: A Guide for Christian Singles* (Orrington: Calvary Chapel Publishing, 2006), 12.

8   John S. C. Abbott. "History of Napoleon Bonaparte (1855)", Chapter 38. Online reference: http://www.yamaguchy.com/library/abbott/bonapart_38.html.

9   Rick Warren, *The Purpose-Driven Life* (Grand Rapids: Zondervan, 2002), 236.

10 Gary Chapman, *The 4 Seasons of Marriage: Secrets to a Lasting Marriage* (Wheaton: Tyndale House Publishers, 2005), 3.

11 Keller and Keller, *The Meaning of Marriage*, 77.

12 We do not use the real names of the people we counsel. We intentionally change certain details in the narrative, while maintaining the core message, to protect their dignity. This applies to every other story used in the book, except our own.

13 Keller and Keller, *The Meaning of Marriage*, 119-146.

14 Gary Chapman, *The 5 Love Languages: How to Express Heartfelt Commitment to Your Mate* (Chicago: North Field Publishing, 1992). This is one of the most practical books about romance ever written.

15 Shaunti Feldhahn, *The Surprising Secrets of Highly Happy Marriages* (New York: Crown Publishing Group, 2013), 25-28.

16 The French teacher job qualifications were for basic French. I am not a certified French teacher.

17 Sherry Graf, *I Don't Get You: A Guide to Healthy Conversations* (Colorado Springs: NavPress, 2016), 19-36.

18 Ibid., 28.

19 Ibid., 15.

20 Elizabeth Elliot, *Passion and Purity: Learning to Bring Your Love Life Under Christ's Control* (Grand Rapids: Revel, 2002), 154.

21 Keller and Keller, *The Meaning of Marriage*, 77.

22 Winnie Waruguru is a personal friend. She shared this poem on her Facebook timeline while doing a series of posts on love and lust. I asked for her permission to use her Facebook updates to edify the saints.

23 Robert L. Crooks and Karla Baur, *Our Sexuality* (Boston: Cengage Learning, 2016), 414. Crooks and Baur cite work by the National Health and Social Life Survey (NHSLS) concerning sexual enjoyment. The specific section is found in chapter 13 on table 13.2.

24 *Lust and the City* is available for free on www.penshop.penstrokes.co.ke.

25 Timothy Keller (@timkellernyc), "Everyone says they want community and friendship. But mention accountability or commitment to people, and they run the other way.", Twitter, April 30, 2014, https://twitter.com/timkellernyc /status/461525634758742016.

26 As mentioned earlier, we do not use the real names of the people we counsel. We intentionally change certain details in the narrative, while maintaining the core message, to protect their dignity. This applies to every other story used in the book, except our own.

27 Richard Baxter, *A Christian Directory: Or a Sum of Practical Theology, and Cases of Conscience* (Urbana, IL: Project Gutenberg, 2012), Chapter IV, Part III, "Directions against Hypocrisy", Direct. XI. https://www.gutenberg.org/ files/41633/41633-h/41633-h.htm

28 Keller and Keller, *The Meaning of Marriage*, 119-146. Referring to Timothy Keller's three levels of friendship as cited in chapter six. We deduced habits that will build a relationship based on the three levels.

29 Fyodor Dostoyevsky, *The Brothers Karamazov* (Urbana, IL: Project Gutenberg, 2009), Book V, chapter 3, "The Brothers Make Friends", https://www.gutenberg. org/files/28054/28054-h/28054-h.htm.

Equip Your Premarital Ministry

There are many resources which can equip your premarital ministry, including some which have been created in Africa. Oasis recommends:

GETTING MARRIED? BUILDING YOUR MARRIAGE BEFORE IT BEGINS
Chao and James Wanje

Marriage is a huge life transition. Luckily, you don't have to do it alone. For over 10 years, James Wanje and Dr Chao Tsuma Wanje have prepared couples to start out their marriages right.

Written as a friendly and light-hearted conversation, this book is perfect for you and your fiancé(e) to read and discuss together. Drawing from timeless wisdom and real-life examples, this husband-and-wife team helps couples to resolve conflicts before they explode.

They tackle topics such as finances, in-laws, sex, and roles. Couples will learn to communicate their expectations and intentionally build their relationship. At your own pace, and in your own space, talk through the discussion questions and bond with your partner. Investing in your marriage before it starts is well worth it.

THE SISTERHOOD SECRET: CHANGING THE WORLD TOGETHER, ONE WOMAN AT A TIME
Levina Mulandi

The Sisterhood Secret expounds on Titus 2 to give women an in-depth guide on how to disciple younger women in all areas of life. In *The Sisterhood Secret*, Dr Levina Mulandi casts a vision by telling stories of some of the 50 women in Nairobi, Kenya she has discipled.

More than Bible study or a church program, Dr Mulandi shares how she empowers any woman to mentor younger women, guiding them to understand their identity, discern the purpose of their lives, and be transformed to be more like Christ. The women that Dr Mulandi has walked with have mentored dozens more through this life-on-life discipleship model which is a family relationship between sisters in Christ.

A PRE-MARRIAGE COUNSELLING HANDBOOK: FOR PASTORS AND LAY COUNSELLORS
Alan & Donna Goerz

A Pre-Marriage Counselling Handbook was written specifically for the African context on how to build a successful marriage. Covering topics such as:
- Getting to know your spouse
- Communication skills and conflict resolution
- Marriage vows
- What the Bible says about sex
- In-law relationships
- Financial home management
- Preparing a godly home for children
- Building a biblical foundation

Designed as a seminar-in-a-book, *A Pre-Marriage Counselling Handbook* equips pastors and counselors to teach biblical pre-marriage classes and seminars.

OASIS INTERNATIONAL PUBLISHING

oasisinternationalpublishing.com I oasisinternational.com

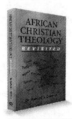

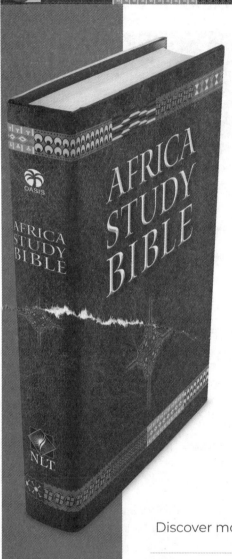

SATISFYING AFRICA'S THIRST FOR GOD'S WORD

OASIS INTERNATIONAL
is devoted to growing discipleship through publishing African voices.

Engaging Africa's most influential,
most relevant, and best communicators for the sake of the gospel.

Creating contextual content that meets the specific needs of Africa,
has the power to transform individuals and societies, and gives the
church in Africa a global voice.

Cultivating local and global partnerships in order to publish
and distribute high-quality books and Bibles.

Visit **oasisinternational.com** to learn more about our vision,
for Africa to equip its own leaders to impact the global church.

oasisinternational.com

oasisinternationalpublishing.com

godswordforafrica.com